Live

a polemical review
of the performing arts

Live

food for the soul

a new generation of british theatremakers

interviews by david tushingham

photographs by simon annand

Methuen

First published in Great Britain in 1994
by Methuen Drama
an imprint of Reed Consumer Books Ltd
81 Fulham Road, London SW3 6RB
and distributed in the United States of America
by Heinemann
a division of Reed Elsevier Inc.
361 Hanover Street, Portsmouth, New Hampshire NH 03801 3959

ISBN 0-413-68790-2

A CIP catalogue record for this book
is available at the British Library

Phototypeset by Wilmaset Ltd, Birkenhead, Wirral
Printed and bound in Great Britain
by Cox & Wyman Ltd, Reading, Berkshire

contents

Most books about theatre are concerned about the past, describing famous productions and evaluating careers from a safe historical distance. They discuss work whose value is beyond dispute for the simple reason that it can never be seen live again.

This situation is widely at odds with theatre practice. Live performance derives much of its excitement from its uniquely ephemeral nature. No matter how many rehearsals and previous performances there have been, each new audience presents a different challenge. There is no one, definitive performance. Each performance of the same piece will invariably be different. What opens as a triumph may turn into a failure – and vice versa. The thrill of the moment, which gives the theatre its attraction and its power, also makes it a highly unstable art form.

In the light of this situation, *Live* has been conceived as a means of offering informed debate about what is happening in the theatre now **and where it may be heading in the future. This first book consists of a series of interviews with a variety of people currently producing some of the most innovative work in the British Isles. These dialogues are intended to offer insights from within a continuing creative process, rather than polished gems of wisdom. As Heiner Müller has said on a similar occasion, interviews are themselves another kind of performance.

Some interviewees may appear to contradict each other (and even on occasion themselves). That they are prepared to do so confidently and unacrimoniously is indicative of a period in which the British theatre is advancing in a number of different directions simultaneously. The potential for diversity which has always existed within the theatre is now being realised in the programmes of an increasing number of venues throughout the country and enjoyed by a wide variety of audiences.

This is an auspicious moment to be launching *Live*. We hope that this and future issues will stimulate and encourage readers to explore and further this process.

jeremy weller
I see the world as a casting room

Jeremy Weller's productions for the Grassmarket
Project in Edinburgh include *Glad* (1990), *Bad* (1991),
Mad (1992) and *One Moment* (1993). Each of these
shows had a cast of non-professional actors. He has
also directed and devised *Pest* (Volksbühne am Rosa-
Luxemburg-Platz, Berlin, 1992), *13 Hamlets* (Schauspiel
Bonn, 1993) and *The Foolish Young Man* (Münchener
Kammerspiele, 1994), for which he was about to start
rehearsals when this interview was held.

Jeremy Weller (right).

In Britain, especially in Britain, probably in the whole of the western world, there's a controlling aspect to all art. The romantic myths, all art, has traditionally been controlled by the establishment – and I find that very obnoxious. I'm not interested in it. I want to look **underneath** that. Because I don't essentially believe that art is a hierarchical thing. I believe that all art is available to people who have a capacity to feel. And if they can feel, they can understand it. They don't **need** to be educated.

A major thrust of your theatre pieces is to introduce audiences to worlds and experiences to which they are not normally privy, to introduce them to parts of the world where they live with which they have lost contact . . .

When I take twenty young boys that eighty per cent of the audience has never encountered, that there have been headlines about, that there have been over-dramatised stories about . . . And you **see** them, you feel them near to you . . . And you hear about their **lives** and you see them representing their lives . . . There's a special knowledge that can be given. A really useful thing can be passed on. If you sat down here with a boy from prison, a child molester who's in prison for attempting to kill a six-year-old boy . . . When you sit here you have another revelation of this person: what is he like as a human being? what is he like beyond his characterisations? That's the kind of thing that excites me.

That physical proximity is becoming increasingly rare, the longer we're used to having televisions not only in every home but in several rooms in most homes . . .

Part of the problem for me of television is that it fictionalises everything. You see something like an American soldier being dragged through the streets and it becomes an experience equal to that of watching a commercial. Television is a terrible leveller.

How is it possible that a nation of 58 million people have allowed a representation of a life to exist which doesn't represent them? The whole organisation of television assumes that there are professionals who can select our images for us. It is a standard strategy of television documentaries to consider the lives of 'ordinary' people but such considerations are normally determined in advance. We look at that couple because they are typical of an upper middle class couple . . . We look at this adolescent in order to understand changing attitudes to violence . . . In every case the individual represents a type understood in relation to an agreed image of society.

That's why, in my work, I use **experience** as a starting point. So that you look at experience and therefore you can break the cliché.

So far in most of your projects you've been interested in groups of rather naive figures, people unclouded by reflection, but governed more by impulse . . .

That's something to do with how I see things now. I do think we're in an intellectual smog at the moment. I mean, what's been the great achievement of the last twenty years in intellectual circles? It's been the destruction of meaning, crushing all meaning out of things, stripping the meaning away from morals . . . Everything's become relative.

And I think our instinct has been crushed out of us as well. Normality has really become a fascistic thing. All round the world, people have very clear ideas about what normality is now. And quite clear ideas about how to conform to it – whereas these different groups of people perhaps didn't have that norm. They had to find their way with the barest of instincts to **Life**.

It was a way of looking at: what is justice in its rawest sense? Justice in its rawest sense must be when someone has to decide whether he should kick an old man's head in to take his blanket, you know, should he do this? When he wants that blanket, he's freezing cold himself. Or your parents have made you, you believe, become mentally ill but how do you respond to that? Do you forgive them or do you try and destroy them?

It's the rawest element of what justice is, what honour is, what dignity is, to look at that. When you have nothing else and just your instincts, what are you like? If you strip all the civilisation away from you, what do you become like? Would you kick someone to death to take their coat? What would happen? These aren't silly questions. They're not pretentious statements. People do kick other people to death out there over things like a coat or a pocketful of change. So it's to say: what are these people like? what are the laws of conduct for these people?

And what brought you to the theatre as the place or a form to do this in?

I only work in theatre because I want to discover about **Life**. And the experience element, for me, is a way of discovering something about Life. I don't have any great allegiance to theatre, but it is possible for me to excite my interest and make discoveries of a kind that possibly I wouldn't if I just did a production of a known play . . .

I think everything needs shaking up a bit. This can provide a bit of freshness, it can provide more **life**, this can provide another possibility. And that's interesting: you **can** make a play almost about anyone. Human beings are infinitely interesting. It reinstates the interest of human beings in a way, beyond actors . . . I see all the places where I go as like a casting, I see the world as a casting room.

Did the people who you asked these questions actually have answers for you: did they know any more than you did, or did they turn out to have the same difficulties?

No, because there are different rules. British culture divides everything very neatly. You and I – perhaps, if we're lucky – can lead quite an illusory life. **We** can live with our illusions, maybe not having them taken away from us, about what we are: are we a good person, are we a bad person, are we indifferent? Maybe life has never forced a confrontation with these things. The people I met initially, the skinheads, the homeless, the young criminals, the women with a history of mental illness . . . these people had usually been so far into human experience that they'd confronted what they were and what the possibilities of their lives were and so they had a kind of lucidity about **Being**, about what they could do. And so they had rules about what life is and what life means very different to yours and mine. Maybe you've been that path. I've been some of the way, but not as far as these people. Their problems and the things that they face are different because they've thrown away the rule book.

Do you find that people tell the truth when they're talking about themselves?

People sort of give away things and you have to put together the pieces . . . You just have to listen, you have to really listen to what people are saying.

David Mamet once said: 'In the movies, as in life, anyone who tells you what they're like is lying.'

There's something in that. No. People are always **doing** things. That usually gives them away. A combination of what they don't say, what they do say and what they do: you can usually get some sort of middle path and keep them there. Anyway, most of the people, a lot of the people I've been working with so far, are unable to talk their lives out. But they are able to just live their lives and you can see what they do . . .

So far you've done a number of pieces with distinct groups of people: the homeless, young offenders, the mentally ill . . . Have you ever attempted to work with the same people again and produce a second piece with them? Or did you think that every time you'd gone as far as you could with the people involved?

Some people did move forward. Some of the people in *Glad* were in *Bad*. But I genuinely believe that a lot of people only have, say, a couple of parts in them. And these parts are related to the way they've lived all their lives. And that's it. You can't actually get any more out of them as far as spontaneity and freshness are concerned. I've never pushed anyone to a third time because I think they might become an actor then.

Is this a fate you're anxious to save them from?

In a way, yes. Part of the reason people liked *Glad* so much was because the people on stage were so naive as to the response they were getting from the audience. They weren't milking it, they weren't self-consciously drawing things out of themselves. It seemed to be fresh, it seemed to be happening.

Of course it was created so that it looked as if that was happening, but the audience took it completely at face value: Oh, look, this is happening for the first time. And you don't see this element of playing with the audience, saying: Look at this **skill**, aren't I **skilful**?

Yes, but do all actors do that? Are they all **showing off** all **of the time?**

Do you know many actors?

Yeah.

Is it true then, or not? Tell me. When they're good, they're very very good but when they're half bad, they're bloody awful. That's how I see it, I'm sorry. I'd like to say nice things, that I love actors dearly. And I do. If they have the experience. That was the point. I don't care that they're an actor, that doesn't bother me, they don't have to be an actor and then I say: Well act this experience. It's a question of **experience.**

Do you find it difficult to get people who you're interested in to reproduce features of their behaviour which you find interesting? Do they get kind of self-conscious about it, do they get coy about it?

Well that's up to me to create an atmosphere where it's very natural for them to reproduce what I've seen or what I know is there. That's a long and hard process. But in general, no, they don't. There's not a trick in it, I'm just saying: What do you do in these circumstances? And they just show me. And often when they show me it's just so . . . the imagination can hardly grasp it, it's so complex. I was reading about Daniel Day-Lewis: he was saying in preparation for his Gerry Conlon he's having buckets of cold water thrown on him. He's **paying** people to shout at him, he's living in a cell on the set, on the film set.

(Laughs.)

I know, exactly. I mean, I had to laugh my head off. He's not responding to Daniel, he's responding to Gerry **only**. And I just thought: What Is Going On? And he hopes to get some sort of great depth there! Maybe in the world of fakery he can reach an immense depth, but I can guarantee you the psychological pain of being in prison for a year or six months or four months is **way** past his understanding. I could go in there and find six prisoners who would be better than Daniel Day-Lewis. That's what I would guarantee – and I would put that as a bet to someone, that I could do that. Because you can't replace, you can't possibly replace **Life**. Gérard Depardieu can play a very good criminal because he was a wild youth. He's also a genius. But a criminal can play a criminal without being a genius, he can just be a criminal.

If everyone worked this way, Shakespeare would have had to have been Danish and a murderer in order to be able to write *Hamlet*!

If Hamlet had written *Hamlet*, it would have been a very different play. I don't think that Shakespeare would have had to have been Danish and literally his father have been murdered, but I think it's interesting when you meet people who've had a father murdered or a sister or a brother and then you question them about how they see *Hamlet*. That's a very different viewing to an actor's. There are other ways of looking at *Hamlet*.

I thought about a version – I had, well, my sister was murdered by her husband four years ago. And I thought, well, how does Hamlet **feel**? And I think he wants to do two things. I think, one: he wants to put the world right, that is, clear the slate, have some sort of moral control over life again. But he also wants to kill himself. He really does. I believe that *Hamlet*'s really the story of someone struggling specifically with their conscience and looking at the world where conscience isn't important, where people can just go on and push things under the carpet.

If I did a *Hamlet* I would probably do something about a bit of my story, about my sister's murder and how I feel as someone involved in theatre, what I want to do. Because I understand the desire to kill. I can imagine getting in my car, driving to where the murderer lives – he only got two years in prison – and I can imagine killing him. And I'm supposedly a civilised person, educated, reasonable.

One thing I wondered, looking at some of your shows, was whether you strive for a certain unprofessionalism in the direction? As a sort of trade mark to let people know: these people really aren't actors.

Have you seen *Mad*?

I didn't.

See *Mad*, then you'll probably have another opinion. Because in *Mad* I had quite a few actresses. Because the only criterion for getting into *Mad* was that you had to have a history of mental illness. So lots of actresses turned up, of course. Now that is a **tight** show. And people say, you know, it works very much as a piece of theatrical art because it's so tight. But I think there are limits to what you can do. What I can do, I do – and that's all there is to it. If I could have done more with the old folks in *One Moment*, I would have.

The most splendid moment on the night I saw was when one woman laughed out loud when another of the performers did something wrong. And her face lit up, she let out this huge belly laugh – and then she suddenly remembered that she was supposed to be acting **– and she got terribly embarrassed, did this enormous double-take and sat down, mortified. The entire evening was worth it for that moment.**

That for me is the equivalent of going to see the Royal Shakespeare Company and a bit of the set falling down. And everyone goes Ooh! Or the window won't open on Don Giovanni. Everyone goes: Aah, what's going to happen? And the actor says: Well, I suppose I'll have to sing that again . . . But those moments are able to happen in my work because I say it doesn't matter. I say to them: If someone does something and you find it annoying or you want to say something extra, say it – if it's true to the moment when you're there.

My suspicion is that to a lot of people who work professionally in the theatre, your work seems very complicated: you have to get all

**these special people in who aren't actors and then you go and find
somewhere which isn't a theatre, you seem to do it all the hard way
. . . And in fact it's really something rather simple which might be
considered as masquerading as very sophisticated.**

I think there's an element of sophistication in the way that things are put
together but the actual process is, really it's just so down-to-earth. One of
my major concerns is that I take theatre out of theatre. I think the idea of a
specialised theatre audience is ridiculous. I also have a problem with
political theatre, theatre that becomes agit-prop or serves some kind of
orthodoxy or a group . . .

**Having said that, I think a lot of people who've seen your shows
might claim that that was what you were trying to achieve.**

Take something like *Bad*. People said: You worked with criminals, that's
what you did. I didn't actually. What I did was I set myself a question. I said
to myself: Is it possible for this group of boys to find redemption? That was
what I asked myself and I actually went through the whole project trying to
answer that question. And I answered it partially. It is possible for rare,
exceptional boys to redeem themselves or be redeemed. But these rare boys
were one in five hundred because the circumstance they lived in was like a
trap and there were very few ways out. It was a culture within our culture, a
very strict culture.

I always ask a question. In Munich, for instance, this young boy takes all
these people into his room and I'm asking: Is it possible to do this? Is it
possible to lead a completely moral life? Or what you believe is a completely
moral life? What happens to you? And that's what I want to try and find
out.

**In asking these questions, what is it that you feel you're offering the
audience?**

What I'm offering the audience is the effort. The effort of going through all
of these things has been done for them so that they can go on this journey of

discovery. All they have to do is actually be present emotionally to find out what the journey meant and whether there is a conclusion to it.

Are you offering them a sort of distillation of your experience?

As near as I can to my experience plus the experience of the people themselves.

Or are you trying to set them off on the first step of their own . . .

Ideally, ideally. Basically you're saying am I a moralist?

No. I'm saying: Do you feel sufficient confidence in the theatre as such that doing shows like this . . .

I do actually.

. . . is sufficiently constructive or could be sufficiently constructive that going to see them really helps people? Or do you feel that it can only be a first step to going further in their own lives and changing**?**

It's down to their own lives. They can go on this experience with me, whatever it is, whether it's *Glad*, it's *Bad*, it's *Mad*, or *The Foolish Young Man* in Germany, they can go through this experience, but the change, if they wanted to do something themselves . . . This boy risks his whole life to bring all these refugees and people off the streets into his room. Everyone: his family, his tutor, professor, girlfriend, all say to him: What the **hell** are you doing? He says: I don't want to live my life in an illusory way, I want to do something, just do something, I don't want to be paid back for this, I just want to do **something**. Everyone tries to turn what he does into something else to suit themselves. The audience can go along with that, and maybe they can judge him and say it's stupid, it had to end in disaster. But in another way it might actually help **them** to try something.

simon mcburney
The celebration of lying

Simon McBurney is an actor, writer and director, and co-founder and Artistic Director of Theatre de Complicite. He has acted in over a dozen Complicite productions and has directed their last two shows, *The Street of Crocodiles* (1992) and *The Three Lives of Lucie Cabrol* (1994).

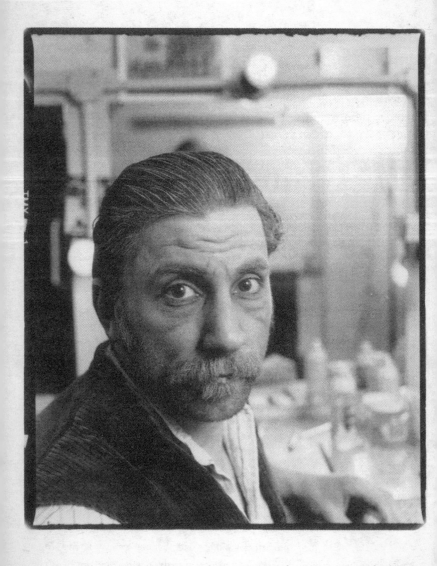

Where did you get the name Theatre de Complicite?

I think the Oxford English Dictionary definition is 'partnership in an evil action'. The idea of partnership in some shared piece of wrongdoing is something that's always pleased me very much.

Philippe Gaulier always used to say that when he sees a piece of theatre he would like to feel a complicity between the actors on stage – not only between the actors on stage but between the actors and the audience. So there is a common joke, if you like, a sense of common understanding which exists in that room for the evening. And part of the actor's job is to be able to stimulate that within the centre of the audience. You celebrate the fact that the audience is there – without them you're not going to make a completed whole.

Unless the performers on stage were in greater control of the material they were performing or had in some way had a more creative hand in it than was generally accepted, this sense of shared understanding was not palpable. So I deliberately set out to work with people collaboratively. It seemed the obvious way to work, to me. It seemed the natural way within the context of the theatre. To wait and be told what to do seemed to me to be the unnatural thing. Our principal aim was to make people laugh through incredibly simple resources, that is to say, almost absurd resources. At the same time, the themes that we took, the ideas that we tackled, were very close to ourselves. They were personal and urgent ones.

At the beginning all of these elements were both confused and interconnected. With hindsight you can separate them out and place a structure over all of them, but in many ways it's just a random series of events. As an artist you look at the world and you try to make some sort of order out of it, whether it's through comedy or whatever it is. But I would say the elements of what we're doing now were in place with the very first show that we did, some of the ideas, the perception of the world around us.

And basically you were a group of performers presenting devised pieces and developing those as you went along.

Right.

And learning from the audience.

That's right. They would be in constant development and by the time it hit the first night, you know, it was a total mess but, on the other hand, that wouldn't faze us, we'd just carry on until it started to cohere. So the ethic was one of continuous work rather than designed product. Which was antithetical to the way the majority of people work in theatre.

What was curious was we were making people laugh out of really extraordinarily odd circumstances and situations . . .

Odd in what way?

Surreal and painful. The themes were urgent ones. The show *A Minute Too Late* was a show which was directly conceived out of bereavement. For me it was a kind of working out of my father's death. And yet there's never been a funnier show.

The piece after that Neil Bartlett directed and that was a terrible fight to get that on. That was with Tim Barlow, who's deaf, and the three of us crazy actors . . .

More Bigger Snacks Now.

It was about not having money and places to live . . . trying to capture what we felt at the beginning of the eighties. And the quality of defensive aggression which we managed to convey within this show was, I thought, kind of spectacular. And it was very, very funny. It was **extremely** funny because we were just four people who sat on stage and we argued and dreamt together and assaulted the audience and nothing really happened – other than we managed to convey a sense of enormous subconscious **desire**, unformed desire.

A lot of the early shows were about the raw physical sensation of different emotions. What was curious was that people would laugh, roar with laughter and enormous numbers of people would weep too because they just found something about the quality of the energy . . . Particularly if they were people of our age and they recognised absolutely what we were talking about, there was something very true about it. Because everything we did was based on observations of things we could actually see and feel, combined with wherever our imaginations would take us.

It's quite a while ago now and I have some difficulty remembering what the theatrical landscape of the time was like, but I remember your early shows with great fondness. Because a lot of the other new work that was around was to do with plays and presenting a play and you went along really first and foremost to decide whether it was a good play or not, rather than to have an evening out. And when you saw a Complicite show it was more like going to a concert. You would see actors jamming on stage and yet producing a kind of theatre which somehow managed to be much closer to one's own experience and one's own life than a number of deliberately written pieces. Did you feel it was an advantage as performers to be able simply to make up your own parts as you went along?

You know, I don't think we ever asked ourselves whether it was advantageous or disadvantageous. I think we just did it because that was what we did. We played together – and we looked at the world and it would make us laugh and it would make us cry. We'd get in and we'd shout at each other in the rehearsal room and then we'd have these frenetic bursts of energy, you know . . . And then we'd have an absolute riotous day where we'd laugh like crazy. And then we couldn't get anywhere and we'd kind of sit around banging tables and chairs for hours on end and then gradually somebody would come up with a character, just kind of out of desperation. And then somebody would play with somebody else and gradually these fragments would **emerge**.

Peter Brook talks about having a hunch. I quite like that. I think it's in *Shifting Point* where he says all he has when he starts a piece is a hunch. I think very often that's all we had. It was out there somewhere . . . It was not a particularly great time, the beginning of the eighties, it was rather a hard moment. So there were a lot of rough edges, but I think that was very advantageous. We would sort of construct a playground in the rehearsal room and then out of that playground things would start to emerge and the pleasure of it was a crucial element, the pleasure of that creation. Then as the date for performance got closer and closer the necessity to have something to show for it became ever more urgent, so, yeah, jamming together is a good way of putting it.

We felt closer to performers on a comedy circuit than people in the theatre. I remember our very first show at the Almeida, we just jumped into a taxi after having done it, went to Jongleurs and ripped bits off, did them on the stage with Arthur Smith and Rory Bremner. I think that was very healthy because it kept us in touch with a vital outside which is extremely important, it sort of kept our feet on the ground. My background was a kind of academic one, so it was a relief to do something that didn't have anything to do with that.

Did you actually consider heading more for the comedy circuit?

Well, I had already sort of decided that wasn't what I wanted to do. Because I had already been asked to do that. And in some senses, by going off to Paris I left that behind. I don't know, comics have this weird life and most comics at some stage reveal that they want to do something serious. So I thought: Before I get too much into that, I think I'll try and integrate those things straight away.

One of the things you did in Paris was study with Lecoq . . .

I learned a lot of things, he's the most wonderful teacher. What I learned most of all I would say is . . . There are two things, really. One is an analysis through the use of movement of how a piece of theatre works: how it actually functions in terms of space, in terms of rhythm, almost like music in terms of counterpoint, harmony: image and action, movement and stillness, words and silence. And having clarified the scaffolding of the building of theatre, he was a wonderful teacher in the stimulation of his pupils' imaginations and the celebration of their individual different imaginations within the context of theatre. So that you felt that you came out with the means to express yourself theatrically. And that's very special.

Every single week you had to produce a piece of theatre on whatever given theme. For two years. In a group of people that you absolutely hated.

But you **had** to produce a piece of theatre. Some of those weekly pieces were some of the most amazing things I've ever seen, absolutely inspiring. And so his school was more like a kind of art school in its breadth and range of interest and observation, much less like the theatre schools that I have come across here.

It was very interesting when Celia Gore-Booth was there in the late sixties. At that time even the pupils in his school were affected by '68 and like a lot of students at that time they turned over the whole school and they refused to work. And they said to Lecoq, we don't want to work, we want to teach ourselves. And Lecoq, who's the constant responder and observer, said: Every day for an hour you will teach yourselves. And it was called *autocours*. And that remained in his school and still remains a very important part. There is a part of the day where you are obliged to get into a group and work out what it is you're being taught, which I find fascinating and that was a most marvellous part of the school, very very stimulating.

Coming back from Paris, those were tools which I was able to pick up and handle, which of course were invaluable. I wanted to make the sort of theatre I wanted to make, I wanted to work, as far as I was concerned I was **going** to work, so we got on with the work and we did it. And just through the act of working you generate material and gradually something happens.

And who were the others that you started with?

It started with three other people: one was Annabel Arden, she's my oldest collaborator because we collaborated at Cambridge on such obscure texts as *Sejanus: His Fall*, one of Jonson's lesser tragedies – I must be one of the very few people in the world who's actually played in it; Fiona Gordon, who's a most wonderful comic performer, Canadian, and she has a company in Belgium with her partner – Dominique Abel – called Abel & Gordon and they produce these very strange and wonderful clown shows; and Marcello Magni, who's phenomenal really, he's now established himself outside of the company as well as inside it in this country.

And in the beginning it was a project for a year. And then it grew into a second year and into a third and into a fourth. Then with each show I thought: Well, we'll give it up now. And then another one and then I thought: We'll give it up now. And then a season and I thought: Well, that's enough of that. And it just sort of went on . . .

It really is very remarkable that you've gone from being very, very small scale to a global touring operation. And it's possible to perceive a continuity in the work right from the beginning and yet it's also grown and become much richer and – in the case of the last couple of shows which you directed – much more symphonic.

Yeah. It's really trying to find a language which can accurately represent what you deeply want to talk about, I think. If I wasn't doing that, I wouldn't really be interested in doing theatre. I mean it really doesn't interest me to be developing an ordinary programme. It's very difficult for people to work with us because very often we don't know what we want – the point is we're trying to **find out** what we want. You know, it's a movement which is going outwards rather than towards a single point. If we knew where we're going—

You'd stop!

A lot of people, their aim is very very clear. But for me, you know, I'd like to keep on searching. And now there are books that I would like to make into theatre, books which you wouldn't think **could** be theatre initially, which I think would be fascinating theatre. And there are plays that I would like to do. I think it's very hard sometimes to do classics because you're constantly trying to revitalise them. You've got to be absolutely sure **why** you want to do them. We were very sure as to why we wanted to do *The Winter's Tale*, so that gave us a very particular spur. I think that we should do some Chekhov at some point, I think that that's very close to us, the comedy of it. I don't know when, maybe not until the end of this century.

Are you at all conscious of being an English company or a British company? Or do you feel that you're a European company?

I like working with international casts, it always begs the question why. Some people find it rather self-conscious maybe that you work with foreign actors. Well, it so happens that I know a lot of actors who are not British – it's just whoever's right for whatever role. Whilst in Paris for three years I came across such an enormously broad spectrum of actors from all over the world, it continued a sense of openness towards ideas, style, experiment. You were never falling into a particular avenue. People were always coming up with something you never expected because it came from a different basis.

One of the things I think which makes some people frightened of working with actors from different countries is the verbal element in theatre and you've been very upfront about letting people speak their own languages in performances and letting the audiences cope with it.

In *The Three Lives of Lucie Cabrol*, because Hannes Flaschberger is from Carinthia, from mountains in the southern Alps close to the border with Yugoslavia and Italy, when he uses his own dialect you feel the weight of the place. It has a musical quality which is absolutely right and when he finds it and plays it right then the audience understands what he means. So their head is bypassed and it speaks directly to their hearts. And that's what's absolutely crucial for me in the theatre, is that people should not only be there for their intellectual experience.

That's why what I liked about *The Street of Crocodiles* was people would come out saying: I was moved to tears and I didn't know **why**. That was right for me, that was the right way round.

I think it's a very liberating experience as well because I certainly thought: Well, yes, I can understand Spanish suddenly. And of course I couldn't translate it, but I did feel that I knew what people were saying in particular situations. So I think that's something that works very well, it seems a very natural thing, that internationalism, it doesn't seem to be something forced.

When you're composing a piece, it takes an enormous amount of time to believe that somebody speaking their own language would be right and only that would work at that moment. And a lot of questioning. And sometimes I'll take a lot of the foreign language out of it before it comes back in again.

It fits together as well with the material you're interested in.

Of course.

And what the people are writing about: Bruno Schulz, John Berger . . .

He would see himself as a European writer, now, rather than a British writer.

. . . and Daniil Charms. But I think one of the things which binds these writers together with your earlier work is a curiosity and interest in the individual lives of very ordinary people, and their particular fates and emotions and concerns. You're not presenting people with a very self-conscious power to shape a great deal of the world. And I wonder whether this matches the means that you choose, that if you want to do that kind of overtly political play it needs to be more rhetorical, more to do with making big speeches and things, while your interests lie in another direction?

The humanity of the people that we deal with is very, very important to me. In the early work – and it's still the same now – I'm fascinated by the detail of everyday life, the mundanity of what we live. It's all very ordinary, it's not extraordinary. And what is extraordinary is our internal lives and that's always been a big concern for me: the gap between the internal and the external. It was brought to a head as a concern in *The Street of Crocodiles*, because that was the subject matter: the breadth of the imagination and the way that the imagination works.

When one talks about the political nature of the work I think that you've also got to talk about the politics of the imagination, the way that things are represented. Now, you might write a very political piece for the National

Theatre and make it into a trilogy but I don't know how political that is. Sometimes I think it can be more political to make people dream a bit than to be able to actually articulate a critique, operate a critique. *Ubu Roi*, a completely meaningless piece of nonsense, was highly political at its opening, with the audience beating each other over the head – as are bits of Beckett.

You only have to look at all the different things which have been banned at various times by various people to see that what actually has political meaning is a very diverse area of material.

I think that you have to change the form of theatre for it simply to survive and to grow. The Living Theatre, Brook's fascination with Grotowski and the Wooster Group in New York are all elements which one hopes have changed our theatre for ever – in the sense that in order for theatre to be reclaimed it must celebrate its **difference** as an art form from television.

I think it's interesting to see the criticisms of what we do. People are critical of theatre which plays a lot with images, with bodies, with movement. Yet when you're on stage and it's the body that expresses you're on the side of a mountain, so that it's possible to enter into that place and understand those people and the way that they live – the excitement generated among the audience – the people that I've talked to – it's close to that of children. My newsagent talked about how it was wonderful in *Lucie Cabrol* when they walked over the mountain at the end. I think one critic talked about us walking over the back wall of a house. There's the difference in perception. He **saw** the mountain. That's the politics of the imagination. Although there's nothing there but a plank, you say: Let's **imagine**. And then people do imagine – if you do it in the right way, people go with it in the most wonderful form.

For many years I think some of the most exciting work in theatre has happened in dance and what new dance has done is taken some of the most exciting things of theatre and appropriated them. What theatre's failed to do is failed to respond and say: Listen, this is our language too, the language of the body is also our language. The actors and actresses people have most been excited about in the last ten years have been tremendously physical. Think of the reaction to people like Antony Sher or Fiona Shaw. It's because their bodies are actually **alive** and one hundred per cent engaged in the activity.

And it's their instrument, it's like the best piece of scenery you could possibly have, you can use it any way you want.

The art of theatre is to be able to communicate with the audience. Often people say: I think that's a wonderfully restrained performance . . . I've been along to some of these performances and there's **nothing** happening. There's no connection between these people and what's going on on stage, with the audience – there's no generosity, there's no language. It's the language of television and film, which is wonderful in its own place but not in the theatre.

The theatre's the most wonderful piece of **artifice**, it is fantastically artificial and that's what it's about. It's a celebration of that artifice.

And that's why you keep reinventing all the time, that's what people are looking for. Normally they're only going to see something once, so they want it to be special.

I think the pleasure of theatre is impurity, it's the magpie quality of people stealing from everybody else. It's the celebration of lying: everybody's out there **lying**! None of it's true! Let's get together and enjoy the fact that it's **fake**! And then we're all tremendously moved by it.

bobby baker
Food is my own language

Bobby Baker trained as a painter but soon started to
present performance pieces featuring edible works of
art. In 1980 the first of her two children was born, and
she did not perform again until *Drawing on a Mother's
Experience* (1988) marked her comeback to live art.
She has since completed the first two parts of her
Daily Life series, *Kitchen Show* (1991) and *How to
Shop* (1993), both of which were LIFT commissions.
We met in her kitchen.

I come from a Fine Art background, painting, and I found myself completely alienated from that whole scene. I very much didn't **want** to fit into the way the work was shown and the art world operates. I still find it completely alienating, that atmosphere and hierarchy. I had a whole range of experiences and I hadn't seen any work like the ideas I had. I didn't fit into— I mean I couldn't fit it into a **painting**. I really tried. I did endless, endless paintings. And I didn't know anything about performance. I'd been to the theatre I suppose three or four times. I went to see *Macbeth*. Is it *Macbeth*? The one that – oh, God, this is so embarrassing – what's the one that's got Iago in it?

Othello.

Othello, yes. I was doing that for O-level. Anyway, I fell in love with Iago and I wrote to him. It's the only time I've ever written to anybody. (*Laughs.*) He didn't write back and I thought: Oh, bugger that. I was only fifteen. Anyway, it rather put me off.

I've always been on the outside of what other people are doing. I seemed to be rather preoccupied when I was at St Martin's, so I didn't **see** any of the work that was going on. I don't know how I **missed** it. I didn't go to the cinema . . . I don't know what I did, really, apart from stay in the pub most of the time and drink. And so I developed my own process of working. It was always rather on the fringes of things and working alongside people.

I met performance artists and I kind of got involved in the edges of that. So I did things at places like the Oval House. It was always connected with food. And I just experimented with all these vague ideas. I now realise, looking back, it was actually extremely useful. I experimented in a range of things, which ultimately led me to a very strong conviction about what I wanted to do, but it took a long time. I did masses of different sorts of things: installations, performances in the streets and in theatres and in art galleries, so everything was slightly different to the thing before.

Was that the time you did *An Edible Family in a Mobile Home*?

Yeah. I wanted to make life-size people out of cake. I had made cake babies and a couple of people and it led on to making a whole family out of cake. I got a grant from the Arts Council: there was the Performance Art Committee, they had small pots of money so I applied for £400 and I made this family to inhabit a prefab I was living in in Stepney. I decorated the entire interior in types of newsprint that were appropriate to the person that was in each room. And then I iced it – all over. All the furniture and all the fittings – everything was covered with icing. And then in each room was a different person.

I've got some photographs here. This is the father. And then that's the mother who was mobile. People were served with cups of tea from her head and they ate the family. It was all very polite. A lot of people came – I got children coming in every day – so it gradually disintegrated. This is the son: garibaldi biscuits and chocolate cake. This is the baby: she's coconut cake. She was the only one of the family to actually disappear entirely, in such a brutal way. The teenage daughter was full of meringue. She was suspended above her parents' bed and there were all these very erotic drawings in sugar all over the wall.

Do you eat a lot of cake yourself?

Given half the chance, yes. I don't work with sweet things now but initially I was making everything out of sugar and cake.

Why did you start with those – the sweet rather than the savoury?

The first time was when suddenly I got this idea of making a baseball-boot cake for myself. It was a turning point. I couldn't fit my ideas into traditional art forms and then I discovered my own language. I loved the kind of **gentility** of the cake, the fact you've got this little, very strange, pathetic object that you offer someone. But I did have a real problem with how actually to serve these cakes. I had tea parties when I produced a lot of cake sculptures, but they were rather oppressive. So I discovered things from that and it led on to making more of an impact with an installation.

What I liked about *An Edible Family in a Mobile Home* was the fact that it was completely outside, it wasn't in a theatre and it wasn't in an art gallery, and that I was able to attract a lot of local people because I've always very much wanted to have a connection with as wide a range of people as possible, to actually make the work accessible . . .

I think it's a very nice emblem of your work: that you can give people something to take home with them – or that they can partake of it like some sort of sacrament.

What I found slightly frustrating about it was that it was open for a week and very few people actually observed the transformation and that was such a crucial part of it. It was something I hadn't been able to work out would happen so effectively. It was a devastating image at the end. This family, they were completely destroyed, and it, you know, it actually **smelt** and the walls were . . . It was quite horrifying. And I think I was more distressed than anyone because I'd actually made it as a kind of exploration of my view of family life. What really appalled me was that I'm the youngest member of my family, the baby, and I was the one in this family who was just obliterated. Luckily I've got more optimistic about families since then. But I began to see that I wanted to carry on working outside, in environments or situations that related strongly to people, but to make things shorter. I was seeing the point of theatre perhaps – but coming at it from a rather oblique angle: that you can make an hour-long package and provide people with a whole range of ideas and experiences within that.

Was it after the *Edible Family* that you had your real-life family?

Oh yeah, a while later. I did a lot of different types of work after that, finally producing shorter performance 'packages'. Then I had children and did no live work for eight years.

***Drawing on a Mother's Experience* was one of the very few experiences in theatre where I've been made to laugh hysterically and cry at the same time. I was very struck by your courage and naked honesty in that piece. It was very, very powerful.**

It came out of such a passionate set of feelings, of experiences, that the conviction that I had to try and communicate this with people was very strong. I still find that, performing it. I feel just as angry, just as desperate to explain that process because the things that happened to me and the significance and importance of what happens in daily life isn't looked at and acknowledged.

It took me a long time to work out the form of that piece and what information would go into it. Obviously it comes very much from my interest in painting. And also it was essential that the painting was made of food, because food is like my own language. Food has this wonderful endless way in which it can be used: the fact that it can be eaten or thrown on the floor – or I can eat it – or other people can eat it. It has such possibilities. So that was the obvious thing to draw with and I just loved the idea of doing something like a painting in public, rather than to do it in a studio, but to actually act it out or paint it in front of people. And then to use foodstuffs that reflected a whole range of things that happened, were happening in my life and still happen.

I'm still quite surprised by the strength of the image. It's framed, it's put within this sheet on the plastic sheet on the floor, so it's not going to make too much mess. And then the last thing I do is I roll myself up in it to show how you take your past experience into your future life. And I'm absolutely covered in it, from head to toe. But what's so extraordinary: because I've covered the whole sheet at the end with a layer of flour, that obliterates the image but it comes through anyway on the other side, this spectacular, dripping stain of treacle or blackcurrants or what have you. And then I do this little dance to celebrate the whole experience.

I found that very disturbing, that final image; for me it seemed to be an image of grief, sackcloth and ashes . . . It seemed a kind of abasement too, the way you dirtied yourself, smeared yourself.

Well, it was the final taboo thing of throwing food on the floor – but playing with that idea. To actually roll in it and get all besmirched and stained is obviously very shocking. What's interesting about it – and I find it very disturbing – is that people, all the way through, find things funny, hysterically funny. It's on the edge of what's safe and what's not safe and the humour – it's almost the only way to be able to cope with what's happening

– is my reaction to difficulty, but it's also how society, the audience, react to this.

You mentioned that you were aware of having evolved food as an artistic vocabulary for yourself. Were you conscious of that when you went through the experience of motherhood – and do you think that that made having a baby and breastfeeding and all this sort of thing a different experience for you?

When I had small children I found the first few years so shocking, so extraordinary, I couldn't believe what was happening to me, what was actually going on. It left me unable for a while to know how to articulate that or proceed.

One decision I made really early on was that what was important was to actually examine things from the inside out. That to use my own experience was the only valid way to proceed. Everything kind of crystallised. But it took a long time – because it was very difficult to know how to use what I'd observed.

It seems to me every detail, every aspect of our life is so packed with meaning and profound significance. It came together with the idea I had very early on of wanting to make work that related to those moments in time where just for a split second you experience an extraordinarily complex set of realities, associations. I know the first time it happened was at St Martin's where I was standing in the middle of a studio. I tried painting that moment, which didn't work. It's like when you're a child and write your address with the universe at the end and try and go further.

And that's what happened when I had children: it led me to look at things on a much deeper level. What I actually did from moment to moment was sending out a ripple and I felt so angry that that wasn't acknowledged – not just for me, but that our society wasn't observing, valuing and examining that. So what I've done ever since is a developing process, the *Daily Life* series is a way of investigating ranges of issues.

Did you feel that somehow by becoming a mother you had forfeited your right to be seen as an artist?

Oh, yes. I mean I didn't consciously accept that, but that is what happened at a much deeper level. What had happened was I could not allow myself to be an artist because there was absolutely no precedent within my family that I could carry on acting as an individual, from that moment on I should devote myself to my family, my children and my husband. Once I could actually perceive how I come from a history, a long line of really thwarted women, none of whom could do what they wanted, then it was quite easy to change.

It assumes as well a definition of being an artist which is rather draconian, perhaps not especially useful in human terms.

I don't agree. It assumes that the artist is an independent individual with the freedom of self-expression – which does not tally with the traditional view of a mother.

One of the interesting things you said about wanting to do performances in the first place was wanting to see the audience and wanting to see their reaction. What sort of things do you look for in an audience?

It's an extension of the way I relate to people on a daily basis. And it's very risky, I suppose. There was a great risk in opening my kitchen to the public: to be in such an intimate environment where you can't avoid seeing what's actually happening. I've become so bound up with the people during the performances, that I actually think I know them. I quite often see people at a later date and think I've met them and then it comes out they've been in the audience. It worries me, this confessional aspect, the voyeuristic, the exhibitionist side of it: whether it's really connecting with people and how they respond to what's happening.

I find a powerful sense of compassion there. You present yourself as an example of humanity and your work is clearly from your own experience – but we too are examples of humanity and can have lives which are entirely comparable in their ordinariness and their

remarkableness in that apparent ordinariness and I think because of that the audience feels extraordinary sympathy for you.

It's great when that works. I do feel sometimes that there's a sort of sacrificial element to what I'm doing which is so excruciating.

I think it's very generous. I didn't want you to feel that there was anything selfish about your confessions.

There does seem to be this great need or excitement that people experience about being allowed, given permission to look at what is going on within their lives. On one level they love to look at the mundane, superficial details of, say, shopping – their day-to-day experience. I must admit that I'm more interested in where God and sex come in.

You quoted Bunyan's *Pilgrim's Progress* in *How to Shop* and that was a kind of pilgrim's progress through the supermarket: what kind of salvation do you feel might be possible in a supermarket? Do you think it's possible to reconcile spirituality and consumerism?

Yeah. It's possible to bring together spirituality and every aspect of daily life. It's there, you know, it's in every moment: it's just how you acknowledge that fact and discuss it and bring it out.

You now have a whole body of work, which is a very nice position to be in. I hope at some point you'll be able to do some sort of retrospective . . .

That's the aim at the end of *Daily Life* – to do the whole five together.

Do you then have to do death after that?

No. Then I'm going to have a teashop. (*Laughs*.) I've decided I'm going to change tack completely. I don't know . . . I'm going to do painting again perhaps. I'm really amazed because I've been asked by the Museum of Contemporary Art in Sydney to recreate the *Edible Family* and I was completely staggered when they suggested it because it never occurred to me that it could be put together again. It's very exciting. When I first started working I never did anything more than once and I'm amazed now at how stupid I was. I didn't realise that was the benefit of working, of repeating things and learning and adapting, developing as you go along.

Is it difficult, if you place a great deal of emphasis on the truth of what you're doing, to be able to repeat it and then every time that you do it again to be equally true?

Well, I realise now that different aspects of the truth can come across in each new context: that the process of repeating a performance can help you look at the issues each time in a new light. It's the endless search for that split second of connection.

After I'd been touring *Mother's Experience* and then *Cook Dems* for a while I felt that I couldn't control these changing elements from performance to performance on my own any more. That's when I started working with Polonca Baloh Brown. Initially our working process was very informal and tentative – I was wary of losing control. With the *Daily Life* series, she's been involved as co-director. We've developed a very constructive working process. With each show more people are involved – it's great.

Kitchen Show was funded by the drama department of the Arts Council, and the thing about getting money from them is you have to tour a show. I said that I would tour it because I would open other people's kitchens but we hadn't really worked out whether it would be possible to transfer my actions to new settings. And it has worked really well, because of the strangeness of me showing one dozen actions that take place here and taking the audiences' minds to that space, backwards and forwards from where they actually are and what is actually in the kitchen that they're sitting in.

Of course *Kitchen Show* started here in this kitchen. Would you be prepared to take us on a tour of your kitchen?

You've already had the start of it. That's when people arrive and it doesn't change if it's a paying audience or a guest because I immediately offer whoever it is a hot drink. You had real coffee. In *Kitchen Show* here and in Australia and New Zealand they put up with instant – we couldn't get away with that in Europe and America. We have cups and a trolley ready. I've got an assistant, somebody who helps me serve people, and I explain what I'm going to do: that I feel so strongly about this set of actions that I've gone to a lot of trouble to make them public – that I want people to remember the actions, so I'm going to mark them physically, visually, one by one 'about my person'. It's phrases like this which just crease me up, playing in and out of the absolutely bizarre stupidity of what I'm doing. That people are sitting there watching me is so funny – but at the same time it is so packed with meanings. There are references to these meanings, the significance of these actions, throughout the show – but very carefully understated – so that the work can operate on different levels.

When you've got your hot drink, I want to show you how I serve sugar and milk. I have a particular kind of technique. So I explain that technique and in order for people to remember how I do that I bandage my hand in the spoon-holding position – using a particular kind of elastoplast that I always get as part of my first-aid kit. I like it because it's stretchy and I like the colour because it's sort of flesh-coloured, but it's not. I find it very interesting looking at those bandages, their notion of what colour your skin is. Anyway, I fix my hand in that position so that for the rest of the show it's bandaged. It's a rather grotesque image, it makes everything I do afterwards difficult.

The next one is to talk about cooking. It's an action I have, which I do really to impress people when they're watching what I'm doing. And it's the action of balancing a spoon on top of the pan like that and I have to explain honestly that I do this because I have a friend who's a very good cook who does this and I've never really known why she does it, but I think it looks very professional.

Do you think it might make things taste better?

Possibly. She's Slovene, my friend, and I assumed it was a sort of Middle European technique. Finally her mother was staying and I watched and she didn't do it, she just left the spoon on the side. So I asked her and she seemed quite flattered by my attention to this detail and she actually said that she rested the spoon there like that because she didn't like to have the spoon inside the pan. And it really bothered me because I was embarrassed to say: Why can't you leave the spoon in there or why can't you leave it on the side? So it was another few months before I finally asked her and she said it was because of hygiene.

She bought me this, later on. She was a bit offended when I thought it was very funny. It's a spoon-rest. What she uses now.

After being immortalised in your piece!

So I talk about what I'm cooking and show people the colour of the soup in there, tomato soup, for instance – I can get wonderfully excited about the colour of it. So I run backwards and forwards and give people the opportunity to see the whole thing and I lick the spoon constantly. Eventually I take a clean spoon and I fix it in my hair with a blue hair-toggle, so that I've got this little tuft, which I think is rather attractive. And at the end of each action I make a pose, just for a moment, for a fraction so that people can observe the mark. It's an essential part of the performance because it gives people that moment of time to reflect on what's happening.

I see the cooking area is actually up a step here, rather like a stage.
Is that deliberate?

No, actually, it was a mistake by the architects. They suddenly realised that you wouldn't be able to see out of the window—

I see. And you capitalised on it.

Yes. Well, it has given me, since I've been here, a sense of being on a stage. I have this element of exhibitionism. Acting out my life goes on constantly wherever I am and what I like is the playing in and out of that – the changes which are very difficult to cope with in daily life, when you don't want to upset people or embarrass them too much. You can do it in performance much more acutely. I suppose I use it in this performance particularly.

But playing with that side, making fun of myself, setting myself up as absurd, I found it very risky here. I didn't realise how dangerous it would be when I got strangers coming in. I could see quite clearly that a few of them loathed me, loathed my lifestyle, loathed the whole context, resented it, and yet I was actually opening myself to that and inviting that criticism by making fun of myself and criticising myself. When it's happening really close to you it's pretty . . . it's pretty frightening.

The third action is of throwing a pear at the wall in moments of extreme anger. I haven't got a pear here . . . But I actually recommend what not to, because I've done some very violent things in this space. I threw a typewriter on the floor once and I threw a bottle of wine and I actually dented the floor. Here it is – the red-wine-bottle mark. It's how to cope with those sort of furies which seem to be intensified by being in a kitchen or being in a confined space. It's the place I get angriest. So what I do, or what I recommend, is to throw something soft and ripe or edible – like a pear.

Does this mean your kids aren't allowed to eat the pears because they're for Mummy's throwing?

(*Laughs.*) They know when to duck. I demonstrate a particular technique of throwing – overarm, a kind of cricket bowling technique, which I used to emulate when my brother did it, because I didn't like the sissy underarm business.

I throw it at a cupboard painted with vinyl silk so that you can wash it off. I explain the logic and the problem of little bits of pear getting stuck behind the door. The first time I did it, because my hand is bandaged and I can't aim very well, I hit the light fitting and broke it. But I've got it fairly well . . . I won't do it now.

Then that mark is to put it in my pocket as ammunition. I've got on my white overall – it just sits in there, ready.

The fourth one is running water. Actually I'm going to show you this because I'm very proud of this: how I peel carrots under running water with this potato peeler. I like to handle the carrots and have the water running. You shouldn't peel them because apparently there's goodness under the skin, but I do because I like the way they look and I end up with these wonderful smooth objects.

What I love most of all is this feeling just here. There's a moment when the water just hits my wrist when I feel totally transformed, ecstatic. It's such a powerful physical feeling and it seems to make sense: just the it with the water running and the little splashes that run around the place. This is truly what has happened throughout my life. And I try to explain and demonstrate it and then the mark. is to shower myself with water. So I'm drenched and my eye makeup gets smudged and water makes my overalls transparent. It's a cleansing mark.

Then I go outside – which I don't suppose you want to do because it's snowing – to take the wet tea towel and hang it out on the washing line and then I pretend to be a cat. As you see, we've got three black cats. I don't go out in the garden very often but when I do I get this terribly strong thrill about the thought of being outside and being able to move and run and be wild. And this momentary desire to bend down and imagine it: just once I might be a cat, I might just have their grace and their freedom, moving around across the grass. I talk about that and I demonstrate it. I go out there and charge around the garden. (*Laughs.*) Does cause a bit of a stir, locally.

And then I put a black bin bag on my shoulders, which is my favourite mark, because it looks like a cape. I use pegs off the line and come back and show that. I really like the way I show that mark, too, because I'm standing with my back to people and I'm breathless. And it's this ludicrous aspect of me standing with my back to them and them looking at a bit of plastic pretending to be a cat.

So it's building up. It goes through various stages of being funny and ridiculous and getting slowly more desperate.

After that is margarine. I always buy a particular brand of margarine. In fact I always buy Vitalite, Kraft Vitalite light – which you can't get in many countries . . .

You've tried!

Yes, I've opened kitchens all over the place now. We delved through many tubs. Why I buy Vitalite is it's piped in and it gets this sort of ripple across it with a little nipple in the middle and in fact the Vitalite **light** is the best: a fantastic sculptured shape, this frozen moment. Every time you open a new tub you never know – sometimes they're damaged or they've gone askew – so that's a very thrilling moment. And I explain that and then I use it as a moisturiser. I put on a bit extra, since I was described as being middle-aged in Adelaide which really (*laughs*) took me aback. Anyway, so that's the mark.

Then it's nibbling. It's a terrible compulsive habit which I try not to do in public but I suck food between my thumb and forefinger. I wasn't aware of this so much until I started talking about it, particularly to Pol, because she has obviously watched me doing it for years. Hmmm. It's so humiliating. I hadn't realised anybody had noticed. And yet it's so strange to make it completely public. It's a kind of ceaseless compulsion checked.

The mark is an interesting one because it's related to a story of something that happened when I was little, going into a friend of my mother's house and this woman had a baby. I wanted to see the baby and I wasn't allowed in. I didn't know about breastfeeding: it was never talked about. It is extraordinary. I must have been about eight or nine. And I went into this room – I was told not to but I just went in – and there was this woman sitting next to my mother. And it was extraordinarily shocking because her breasts were naked. I'd never seen naked breasts in my life. And what was so extraordinary was this terrific shock and horror – they were very angry and shouted at me to go away – but I had seen that one of her nipples was bright red. I didn't think it was anything to do with the baby. I decided that she'd put lipstick on it and that's what women did. I thought that for some time, so I make this shape with my lips and I put very bright lipstick on it like that – and show it to the audience. So you can see there the way that that connects with the breastfeeding and the compulsive eating aspect.

You can imagine by that stage my appearance is rather desperate, really, because my makeup's run and I've got margarine over my face and my lipstick all smudged and spoons hanging out of my hair.

The next one is praying, saying the Lord's Prayer, which is something that I genuinely – unlike many people – find it important to do. I have to say it when it comes into my mind, otherwise I forget. So when it comes into my mind I think: Right, quick prayer! and so I bend over so I can just jump up in case somebody does come in. I have a problem in the car . . .

Would you be embarrassed if somebody came in when you were praying?

Yes.

Why?

Well, that's my cultural background. It's something that isn't discussed. Spirituality is embarrassing and should be dismissed or hidden. It's alright if you do it in a church but even the churches aren't to do with spirituality a great deal. The sermon quite often is about the Church, that structure, that set of people. So by actually making it very public – what I do is I go and kneel down outside the window with these gardening knee-pads on: that's the mark, it's funny but it's also pathetic. In other kitchens I've had to do it in some really odd circumstances, like kneeling on top of a ladder, in order to get to a window.

Then I come back and I show how I dance to operatic music! While preparing vegetables. How I discovered opera through Pavarotti. I haven't actually ever been to the opera – well, I went once and that was so awful: I went when I was a student to Covent Garden and saw *La Bohème* and had this terrible, terrible attack of hysterical giggles with my boyfriend and we had to crawl out on our hands and knees. I describe that, how because of my bigotry I have never been able to go to opera – I've still never heard a whole one – but I discovered it through Pavarotti and the World Cup.

So I have *The Essential Pavarotti* and I put it on while I'm preparing vegetables here and I go into a very balletic dance waving food around, shaking flour, throwing leaves on the floor and getting terribly emotional about it all, which I enjoy. So it ends up a real mess and I've got flour in my hair and I end up pinning a spinach or cabbage leaf to my overall as the mark.

The one after that is the drawer. I can never find what I want in this drawer because it's such a mess and things collect in here and so if I can't find what I want in a moment what I do is – I'm not going to do it now because the drawer is so disgusting – I just tip it on the floor, the whole lot. And then I sort things out, I just throw things in the right direction, and I talk about organisation and the desire to structure and categorise every object in the house and the ceaseless attempt to maintain order. And that is a sort of goal. I have this image of things flying around the house and in and out of the house and I'm capturing them at various moments in various places. And I mark that by tying some implements round my neck.

The eleventh is the exhaustion – which overcomes me from time to time in various places but more I suppose in the kitchen – where you're so tired you literally just feel you can't walk another step and if you do you will just snap, crack in half. What I've discovered is if you have very short spells of rest you can actually keep yourself going. And I tell stories about places I've done this, just this five minutes, and gone to sleep on somebody's bathroom floor or in a car or what have you. But on the floor here I take one of these cushions and just lie down for five minutes and get this next bit of energy. And I wedge that cushion into my overall as a mark.

And the last one is that of roaming – and it's the one I'm proudest of. It's an ability I have to be able to keep all these actions going together, seemingly ceaselessly, never necessarily completing them. I have this sense of euphoria and delight that they're all happening and they're all connected. I don't need to despair that I haven't completed anything because I'm keeping them all happening like a set of juggler's balls in the air. And when I'm doing it I feel like I'm flying and the mark is putting these wonderful kitchen cloths in my slippers like wings. So I've got wings and I can fly where I want to.

At the end of that, when I've done the twelve, I explain that there's a certain whimsy attached to putting a thirteenth to make a baker's dozen. What I've wanted to do really all along is make these actions public, and the image that all the marks make together. So what I do is stand on a cake-stand. I've got a very good professional cake-stand and I put it on a coffee table in front of the french windows. And there used to be a piano there and my daughter Dora used to play the piano with a friend while I was doing this. On tour we use a recording of them and show their photo. I just slowly revolve round, framed by the patio doors, and play this bit of music, which is very moving, just this funny bit of classical music that nobody can remember what it is. And I carry on revolving, noticing things, dusting the corners, and then get down and go off and leave the room. And that's it.

Thank you very much.

lloyd newson
Dance *about* something

Lloyd Newson is leader of the independent dance collective DV8 Physical Theatre. Under his direction the company has produced a series of highly acclaimed pieces including *My Sex, Our Dance* (1986), *Dead Dreams of Monochrome Men* (1988), *if only . . .* (1990), *Strange Fish* (1992) and *MSM* (1993).

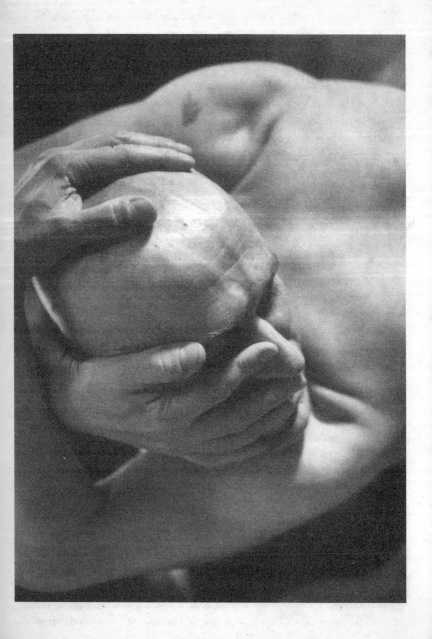

One of the things which distinguishes DV8's work for me is that it's dance about **something.**

One of my concerns in forming DV8 was to broaden the perspective of dance and try and make it more relevant to people's lives. I prefer the term 'movement' rather than 'dance' because I feel that dance is a sub-set of movement. That's also another reason we called ourselves DV8 Physical Theatre, **not** a dance company: because I think 'dance' has many limiting associations.

Too often I see dance companies who are more interested in the aesthetic and the visual than they are in content. Ironically enough, I think **any** aesthetic is political, but unfortunately a lot of people don't take that on board. People refer to DV8 dealing with sexual politics – the Royal Ballet deals with sexual politics, it's just conservative rather than radical. What are the politics of an arabesque? An arabesque does have politics attached to it. It's about perfection, idealism, beauty – an acquired notion! – and in many cases uniformity.

I wanted to open up the realms of what is considered beautiful. The terms 'goodness', 'beauty' and 'success' often become interchangeable. And these in turn produce a very limited range of concerns. These subliminal messages say that unless you look a certain way and are a certain age and can do certain things, you're not good, you're not perfect. It's about forcing very strong romantic notions and highly destructive images of how people should be in order to be perfect or right.

Dance hopefully should be more than acrobatics. Yet to a large extent – and I see a lot of it – it ends up being about what can you do with your body alone, that becomes the preoccupation. DV8's preoccupation is: if the leg is thrown up by the ear, **why** is it thrown up by the ear? There must be a reason for it, rather than saying: Look at what we're able to do. Because that's what happens. A lot of choreographers start off with a theme, be it Dorian Gray or the Extinction of the Planet, and then people come on throwing their legs up in second position or as high as they can lift them. And it's like, what are we talking about here? Anatomical flexibility? Look how high I can kick my leg? Or human extinction?

Physical tricks and virtuosity often interfere with the message being told. To validate our form – because it is one that is constantly trampled upon –

we have to try and show what we can do and what other people can't. This is happening more and more in schools. In order to get funding and because of affiliation with universities, a lot of the dance schools are having to find something they can give marks to – basically it's almost as if the height you can get your leg is equivalent to an academic qualification. What the schools should be doing is paying more attention to the intellectual training of our dancers – and placing greater emphasis on choreography, creativity and individuality.

Art is highly subjective, highly personal and it's about opinions, it's about diversity. That, to me, has been lost, and what we're actually producing, on the whole, are automatons. Dance, more than any other art form, is training everyone towards the same visual ideal. Imagine if every actor were the same size, spoke the same lines at the same time, wore the same styled costumes, moved in the same manner and retired by the time they were forty!

I like to think that the physical language we've decided to explore, while coming **from** the individuals I work with, is something everybody knows about. All the movement that we develop is stylised naturalistic movement. That is, its origins are embedded with meaning – as were most dance forms until they were abstracted out of existence. If someone walks into this café, you have an immediate reaction about the way they look, how they hold their body, what their body's telling you. As a creator, you become aware of that information and you find ways to reveal that formally, stylistically. But its source must always be clear.

There are people in the dance world who believe audiences need to be educated about dance. I feel exactly the opposite. Most dance people need to be educated into the ways of normal living and get reconnected with what the body means to other people, both consciously and subconsciously. When the average man on the street comes and watches a dance performance and women fling their legs wide open, for the dancer it's just a technical event, but for the person watching it it has immense emotional, psychological implications. We shouldn't deny that – nor should we pander to their values alone: art is about challenging. However, we should be aware of the divide and understand what we can do and what that difference means.

**One of the great things about your work for me is the quality of the
acting and I think that comes from your attention to movement.
Because movement is a language which is in many ways less
arbitrary than speech. It's a system of meaning which it's harder to
cheat at, in a way, because movements are all actions, whereas two
words can exchange meanings quite easily: they're much less rooted
in reality.**

Historically, our first forms of communication were with the body and
what we retained were images, long before language was evolved. It is
something I think we retain on a profound level. Images and sensations are
still the things we remember. How often do you leave a play that you don't
know and remember verbal passages?

One of the exercises I do in lectures is suddenly run and jump on
someone in the audience and watch people's reactions. There is something
that happens before the conscious mind is engaged. Studies have been done
where they've monitored audiences, put electrodes on them, and noticed
that the audience reaction is empathetic – they respond physically in
sympathy with the people who are on stage moving – providing they
haven't gone to sleep! There's identification: we've all fallen down, we
know what it looks like, feels like, when you fall backwards . . . you can't
prevent the sympathy sensation, it's immediate.

The visceral aspect of dance precedes conscious thought: that's its
power. But that's also where many new choreographers end their
discoveries. If one can build images, the mind will retain them. Support
them with movement and sensation, the body will remember them.

Although I'm primarily interested in theatre that deals with images and
movement, these have their limitations and more recently I've become
interested in combining them with language. Language has a specificity
which is very difficult to convey just in movement and images alone.

**And it's another ingredient as well. When you have the movement
and the image already there, language is a way of turning that round
and still keeping it. It doesn't destroy it but it adds something and
changes it.**

It can clarify an ambiguity that might exist. Other times the ambiguity is important to maintain and specificity can kill the power of what has been achieved without language. Language just feels like another tool now that I want to have access to. I don't want to lose the power of movement so I'm trying to find that balance – because too often I see a lot of direction where the words attempt to do all the work.

And you see performers hanging around waiting for their next line.

Yeah. I think there has been a definite preoccupation in British theatre with the importance of words. Most of the time when I see text-based work, I leave emotionally unaffected. Because I think that people are still living from their heads and not from their hearts and I think there has to be a combination of both.

Do you think that's a particularly British problem?

I've discovered I can go and watch a dance class with thirty, forty people who I don't know and can tell you who's Australian by the way they move in class: it's about taking space, it's about moving through space, it's about a certain looseness of limbs. I've only ever made one mistake and it was with somebody who was British but had lived in Australia for eight years. So there is definitely something that is physically particular about the British.

At the same time I have been lucky enough to find people like Wendy Houston and Nigel Charnock who have been prepared to take immense risks with me from Day One. People often talk about the trust which must build up between us, because we do a lot of things that people perceive as physically dangerous, and that that must take years . . . People like Wendy and Nigel did it from Day One because there was something in their personalities, the way they speak best about their lives and the world is through performance. It's their mouthpiece, it's the way that they deal with life – so the minute they're performing, the minute they're rehearsing, they've got this urgent and committed voice. They also have a pain that needs to be unlocked. It's not something you build up to – that's **them**, it's there immediately. Often I find with performers if it's not there on Day One, it's never there.

There's been a lot of talk about me getting into people with screwdrivers and sort of trying to prise open their lives. I've found that a lot of our work has been based around people who come along on the first day and say: Here's my life! These people are prepared to reveal everything about themselves in the rehearsal process. It becomes their existence, it's their life, everything about them is apparent in that time – and to find people like that is extremely difficult. A lot of performers I know are not prepared to go through that process of improvisation and self-revelation. It requires from the performer vulnerability, dedication and belief in what it is they're saying. Sometimes I'm accused of not giving the 'key' to release or reveal a performer's talent. Few people take the responsibility to discover their own talents, and wait for someone else to do it. The process is difficult and is hard and, you know, it's not a coincidence that we basically do one piece every year, not six or seven. If you do give out at the level I require, you also need recovery time. What you get on stage with our performers is what they give in life.

You've been very deliberate in setting up the company to avoid it becoming an institution whose inbuilt momentum commits you to producing shows on a regular basis.

I think I'll always find myself complaining because it's extremely difficult, to try and keep that going. When you have to be the producer, the casting agent, the editor, writer and scheduler as well as everything else. But my recent associations with the West End taught me about the conservatism and restrictions of working in mainstream theatre. And it is extraordinary just how much censorship goes on, even if it is covert. It definitely is very much in operation even in the supposedly so-called radical or more adventurous areas of the West End.

It doesn't make you want to go and run the Royal Ballet?

If definitely doesn't make me want to go and run the Royal Ballet. The Royal Ballet is very tied up. They can't provide me with the rehearsal time I would need to do a piece, despite showing interest. So I've found the Royal Ballet very open in one respect of wanting to do more radical work – almost more so than many contemporary companies – but actually not being able to take the steps to truly achieve this. People want the result without making the changes in the bureaucracy that are necessary to achieve this. You can't just get the product without changing the system.

They think all they need to do is just book one or two people and it happens.

Yes, it's a bit like shopping and buying top label clothes, throwing them together and hoping they'll match. Change has to happen on a more fundamental level.

We're not working all the time so we've got to have a publicist you can employ when you can afford it and then not employ. You've got to have administrators who can work full-time and then all of a sudden can cut back to half-time. That creates major problems. But it also enables you to react spontaneously and creatively. Our company is such that we only work when there is something to say or a need to say it. I'm not constantly churning out pieces and I think that that becomes very hard when you're the creator of a major company or theatre, there's pressure upon you to keep producing.

I think that's the dilemma art has got into: the product mentality. It shouldn't be about mass production. Or constant production. For me. I've seen a lot of companies and directors destroyed because market values have been put upon them and all the notions associated with that. So I feel I'm often spending as much energy fighting against other people's preconceived ideas of how I should work and how DV8 should operate. That takes a lot of energy to fight against. But that independence has given me an artistic freedom no institution has yet been able to offer.

DV8 have done a lot of pioneering work in making film versions of dance pieces, and *Strange Fish* has just won a third international award. Are these films a substitute for not having a repertoire, preserving them in a last, ultimate performance?

Well for me the reason we don't have a repertoire is, as I said before, we only create when we feel there's a need to create and it's often around an issue that's pertinent to my life or those close to me at the time. Often the work is a way of exorcising these concerns and once it's done, it's finished for me. To go back would be like going back over old therapy sessions. They were necessary at the time but they're no longer important to re-do. In fact they could be destructive to re-do.

All my work is a personal journey and I can't stress this highly enough: the past work – everything could change tomorrow – is very much based on the individuals who are involved in the production. There's no second cast like there is in most theatre companies or dance companies. There's only one person who does the role and the piece is built around them – around their improvisations, their personalities, the way they look, how they speak. Therefore to find somebody the same . . . For me it's like the analogy of having, say, five or six different chemicals and putting them together. You can't push everyone to be, you know, magnesium sulphate. There will never be two of the same element – so the fusion is always unique. (*Laughs.*) Sometimes you get explosions! Sometimes it backfires in your face because you haven't quite worked out that some chemicals jar with others or that you're allergic to certain substances – but even this is interesting to explore. Our work is about individuals, their lives, interactions and personalities. It's not about: here's the role, the play, the words, the movement – learn it. It's devised work. The work is only ever as good as the people in it.

To go back to the idea of a personal journey, one of the things that I've found very attractive about your work, as someone who comes from the theatre, is that even when you are dealing with a theme, there's very little telling the audience what to think; you don't explain things.

We try to avoid generalising and dealing with stereotypes. For example, in *MSM*, one of my primary concerns – and I only discovered this after doing the fifty interviews – was that each man who cottaged had different reasons, and all had different histories. There was no simple set rule.

I've come to the conclusion that rather than try and have a little sentence that can be handed round at the end of the piece to say, 'This is what it's really about. This is my premise', I prefer to represent people's life, experiences, contradictions and their complexities. Obviously one still has opinions – but sometimes it's more worthwhile to understand a situation rather than judge it.

I suppose in a sense I had to do *Dead Dreams* because Clause 28 had just been passed and I saw Dennis Nilsen as a result of somebody being unable to express his emotions overtly in a society where spontaneous affection between men in public is often open to physical and verbal abuse. This must have a dramatic effect on gay men's psyches. And that's what I felt with Dennis Nilsen. Brian Masters' book is very aptly named, *Killing for Company*. When we looked at and connected our lives to Nilsen's experiences there were extraordinary similarities. The issues were so complex that it wasn't a matter of saying: Well, this man was evil. I was angry that people readily saw Nilsen as a homosexual monster. All these issues are extremely layered and I prefer to represent these experiences from many angles and hope that it will provoke understanding and thought rather than simple moral condemnation.

One of the things that I'm very interested in is the focus that DV8's work has had on sexuality and on emotion and how this has been received, and the fact that you're doing it in a British society which is so screwed up about sex in so many different ways.

My delight is that we made front-page news in two tabloids, one with *Dead Dreams* and one with *MSM*. It has shown and proven to me that movement and dance can be political, that it can have a force, it can affect people and it can create change. And that's what I feel too often dance hasn't done.

People often say: Your work, it deals with gay issues. Well, it does but it also deals with human issues: betrayal, desire, excitement, boredom, confusion. Half the work we've done centres around relationships between men and women. What's been fascinating is how everybody's really focussed on the gay thing. *Strange Fish* was about belief and faith, and what people do in trying to find something or someone to believe in. A lot of our work has dealt with things other than overt sexuality or sexual identity, and I'd like to keep it that way.

There are hundreds of stories out there. There are subjects around that would make fantastic plays and, well, I don't see or hear about many new playwrights that are writing visual or imagistic scripts which go beyond conventional narrative and naturalistic text. Why are theatre practitioners so often doing old plays in traditional forms? One of the things DV8 is committed to is new theatre. And that's all we do: we write and stage all our own work and commission accompanying musical scores. You take a risk doing this because it's not just about reinterpreting an existing script. We not only write these new works, but have to find and devise the languages for them. How many playwrights construct a new language every time they write a play?

I feel that playwrights who simply produce a script and have to wait for somebody else to want to turn it into theatre find themselves in a very weak position. The young directors have all noticed what the critics like and what gets you noticed and gets you a job and that's doing an attractive production of a classic play . . .

I definitely feel in word-based theatre that I do see a lot of people pitching for their careers rather than articulating their life concerns. And until people start doing things for their truth and for their relevance socially, we'll keep seeing work that just operates on the surface, that plays safe. While it might be well produced, it doesn't really speak about now.

To continually keep writing and producing your own pieces is hard. It takes a tremendous amount of work. And you don't earn much money if you're going to work in this way as the work is expensive to produce, the product uncertain and failure-rate high – so you have to accept the costs at all levels. To have the conditions I want and to keep artistic control is more important to me. And unfortunately I can't do work I don't believe in. I can't do it because it doesn't sustain me for nine months of the year.

paul godfrey
Where playwrights are in this country

Where I grew up in Devon, there's a theatre, the Northcott Theatre, and in the early seventies it was run by Jane Howell, who'd been assistant director at the Royal Court. One of the plays that she commissioned and directed and premiered was Edward Bond's *Bingo*, and I saw it there in 1973 at the age of thirteen. There were just six of us in the audience, and I seem to remember the local paper wrote an editorial saying: We want no more of this kind of thing in Exeter. Now that play's a modern classic, isn't it? And I remember by equal chance Joint Stock tried out their productions of *The Ragged-Trousered Philanthropists* and *Cloud Nine* in Exeter and the vigour and vitality of this work made an impression on me at that age.

I've worked for ten years in the professional theatre now, but sometimes I feel as if I've experienced the entire history of twentieth-century theatre. When I left college I got an Arts Council award to train as a director and I went to Perth Theatre in Scotland. There I encountered a kind of regional rep. that reflected British theatre in its pre-1956 state. My first job was to write the poetry for the pantomime, and that was followed by an Agatha Christie play, which that theatre always did just after New Year as the only means they felt to bring in an audience when the snow fell in the Highlands. And from being at that theatre, I suppose I learned the kind of work I wanted to do.

Which was not what was being done at that theatre?

You said that. (*Laughs.*)

From there I went to work in a theatre in Inverness. I got a job which was to research what kind of theatre company could operate there. I went round and met and consulted with between fifty and sixty writers who lived in the area which the theatre was to serve, which was the entire Highlands and Islands, an area the size of Wales. And out of that initial research job I was lucky enough to get to create the company at that theatre. We did exclusively new plays which were commissioned to be performed at the theatre and to be toured throughout the Hebrides, Orkney, Shetland and the north of Scotland. And that work was very successful, I think. It was the first ever professional company based in Inverness and each of those pieces was originated by a writer, created for a specific audience, and the form and nature of each tour was unique to each piece of work.

But doing that made me very aware that I was English and that my work there was as a facilitator. I didn't want to become a kind of cultural colonialist and I decided to return and work south of the border. That was the point that brought me to wanting to write my own play. Working alongside those writers allowed me to recognise that it would be possible to do that.

When you write a play now, what sort of status does it have when you deliver it to a theatre? I'm thinking in terms of how much of the play do you think that the script is capable of representing. Is it the ultimate, finished article or is it a blueprint, a structure to which other people can bring their talents?

I think I'm quite rare among playwrights in that I deliver finished plays to theatres and I won't deliver them until they're finished. Which means there's nothing more to do to them.

Which means you don't do rewrites, basically.

Except I do the most enormous number of rewrites before the moment when the play is finished. And for me the moment when the play is finished means that I'm convinced that every word is the only word possible and the entirely necessary word and there's nothing more to be done. But as a way of explaining I should point out that the play I have recently completed took three years to write and it's a script of around a hundred and thirty pages and I think that I wrote around two and a half to three thousand pages of text, all of which I believed were the play when I wrote them, and most of which had to be rejected. So the finished script that the theatre gets is a very developed and I hope polished, complete piece of work. Once I've finished a play I'm very keen to see what other people make of it.

I've enjoyed collaborations too, librettos and other things. I've even written lines on the spot for actors in the rehearsal room. But that's something else.

Are there particular things that you have learned from using texts written by other people that have influenced the way that you present your work?

Well, I never write any stage directions at all and I rarely ever specify even the locations of scenes. I believe that what you create is an empty vessel. I'm usually surprised by the way they turn out, which is not to say that I don't have a clear idea of the formal nature of the piece, but you try to create some kind of open form that lives when it receives all these other elements.

And that's very often with you producing and casting it yourself . . .

I've had successful experiences when other people have directed my work but I think if you've written the play you have a lot more licence. You can give the actors more freedom too. There's no need to be literal in your interpretation of it, you don't have to be quite so . . .

You feel that often you can produce a braver interpretation or deliberately choose a rather more different world than someone who is trying to understand the text? You know the text already and are seeking to add to it, to broaden it . . .

If I direct my own play, I have the right to go against the text. But I think that if I was directing a play that someone else had written, or if any director directs a new play, I think you have an enormous responsibility to manifest the text. If I've written the play, I have more freedom.

How in fact do you go about creating a new piece, once you have an idea? You've said that the last play you wrote took you three years, which is *The Blue Ball*, which you're going to direct at the National next year. Where do you start when you write a play?

The first two plays that I wrote were very much derived from my experience to that moment. There were elements of autobiography in both those pieces of work. And once I'd spent two years writing plays I realised that I had created a kind of prison sentence for myself, where I would spend the rest of my life sitting in a room writing plays – and perhaps if I wasn't going to be out there in the world any more I would become like Samuel Beckett and the experience I would have to write about would be that of being in a room!

So after those two plays I decided to find a way of using playwriting to extend the areas of experience that I had in my life. The first play I did that way, using research, was *Once In A While*, where I went out and tracked down as many people as I could find who knew Benjamin Britten, and wrote a play about that individual through the different perspectives of all the people that I met.

While I think I have an unconscious idea of the play in my head even before I start the research, these conversations develop that unconscious idea or allow me to clarify it and also extend my knowledge of that particular area of experience and the world. Since *Once In A While* I made a deal with myself which was that I would try and achieve some pieces of work which created the widest pictures of the contemporary world – and each piece would be centred in some fundamental experience.

I also began to think about who there was living who I would like to meet if I were to take the research idea further. I was born at the end of 1960 and in the beginning of '61 the first person went into space; it occurred to me it would be an interesting and absurd idea to track down as many people as I could who'd been in space and see what I could make of that. It seemed to me that it was an experience that hadn't been adequately explored. I had no idea of what it was like for those people and I thought I might be able to find a way to bypass the channels that had been created to communicate that experience. It was a long struggle, raising the money for research trips, getting into the space programmes. Then coming back and trying to create a piece of work that could match that. There can't be many people alive who've met as many astronauts as I have.

And now I'm sitting here and I'm in the middle of another play and I've taken the experience of fear and I'm trying to find a way of exploring the operation of fear, trying to write the widest play that I can achieve on that subject. So the policy now really is to take a fundamental aspect of experience and chase that as far as I can, or until I can find some sort of resolution.

**But this is a policy which you've established yourself, it's not
something which you've been asked to do by a theatre?**

Not at all, no. It's a path I've discovered for myself. I've been fortunate in
that theatres have offered me commissions for plays but I've always laid in
front of them what I wanted to do and so far they've agreed to commission
me to do that.

**Playwrights are the only people working in the theatre at the
moment whose work is compared with everyone who's been
working in the theatre in the past, where the dead are still around as
competitors of the living. Do you feel that this has harmed the way
that you write – or do you see it as a challenge?**

Here in Europe, the tendency is to see the past as a kind of museum, behind
glass, but I find it more helpful to see it as a kind of store in which
everything's there for the taking. Quite recently I rewrote an already
existing play by Henry Fielding, *The Modern Husband*, because I saw a better
way to do it for now.

What's been exceptional about our theatre is the extraordinary quality of
texts that have been produced and if you look around at the theatre here
most of it is remarkable for the nature of the writing. And I know that this
has been challenged and there's a lot of talk of it being text-bound and
there's the notion of physical theatre, which appeals to me – but I think the
real question is: How do you turn words into action? It's churlish to dismiss
the strength that we have in the use of language in our theatre culture. It's a
wonderful structure for a playwright to climb onto.

**What sort of contemporary theatre do you most enjoy? Or do you
find it difficult to go to the theatre if you're writing? Do you prefer to
seek inspiration and kindred spirits in other art forms?**

Well, I wouldn't define myself as a theatregoer. (*Laughs.*) Though I do see a
great deal: dance and performance art as well as plays. Personally, for kicks I
would rather do something like walk five hundred miles across Europe or

go to the first acid house party in Russia to celebrate the end of the Soviet Union or go and watch the Space Shuttle being launched . . .

So are these things experiences which you think a night in the theatre has to compete with?

Yes, certainly.

And do you think it can do that favourably?

Oh yes. (*Laughs.*) I think that for some people who work in theatre, the whole world for them is the theatre. One of the things I like about being a playwright is that, while theatre is the art form that my imagination operates in, I am able to go out into the world and live in the world and explore and then take what I find back into the theatre. And it's deliberate that the work room that we're sitting in, where I've written two plays now, is in this big complex of light industrial premises. I find it stimulating to be here where everybody is making things. For two years I've actually lived here in this office and deliberately put myself at the centre of a city yet away from the areas of habitation within London, as a way of being at the centre of everything but also having a perspective on it simply by not sharing the patterns that everybody else is going through.

So do you think that you live differently now than you would if you hadn't decided to work in the theatre?

Yes, economics is the most important factor here. I think it's very important to recognise your relationship to the society that you're in and what it is you want to do and how that defines your economic status, your situation. I'm a playwright and I have no other form of income and that's what I do. I believe it ought to be possible to live and write plays and that's enough – more than enough – for one lifetime. It takes me all my time and in recent years I've been commissioned by the Royal Court, by the National and the RSC.

Here I've chosen to create a life for myself using the resources I have. I deliberately went out and rented the kind of space that I could afford to live in, which is this office room, which is eleven foot by thirteen with one tap in it. It means I walk around the city and I know: this is where I am, this is where playwrights are in this country. I think it's very helpful to have a clear and deliberate perspective.

And it's also very good practice for writing about life in a space capsule!

Perhaps? (*Laughs.*) I don't know, I don't want to sound sanctimonious about this and I don't want to sound apologetic either because I don't think there's any virtue in poverty. On the other hand I can imagine people who would envy this life.

Theatres are seeking an input from a world beyond the theatre. But at the same time that's something that people often find threatening, if this kind of news from outside does not match up with their expectations. Are you aware in your plays of trying to present a world which can be explained – or of wanting to give an audience a more complex world, to present something to them for which they have to find an explanation themselves?

Let's face it, the mass media exist to inculcate stupidity! There's a tendency to assume that everything can be explained. Those media are devoted to presenting us with easy explanations of the complex experience that we have around us. And I think that any medium that self-consciously chooses to define itself as an art in the way that theatre does has a function to undermine all that and to say that experience is ambiguous and that there is very little that can be simply explained.

And I think that we meet a real dilemma when it comes to the marketing and presentation of theatre where the theatres are now required to meet very high box office targets and are therefore very reliant on critics. Critics obviously tend to recognise work that coincides with their own view of the world which is that of journalism or current affairs. But I believe that the potential of theatre is infinite. And there's a possibility of real confusion where one can aggrandise the current affairs agenda and reduce that of theatre, which could be catastrophic.

I believe that I and many of the playwrights of my generation really struggle with much wider ambiguities than the previous generation, who were defined by their party political affinity. That was something that was obviously much more easy to articulate than the kind of moment that we're dealing with.

What does it actually feel like when you read in the newspapers, not necessarily in a review of one of your plays but in a review of someone's play, that you are working as a playwright at a time which is perceived by a number of critics as a not especially exciting period of British playwriting?

What's difficult is when you have plays which haven't been produced and you devote yourself wholeheartedly to developing the most exciting kind of work that you can imagine and you read in the press material that's as you describe and you're aware that both yourself and your contemporaries have been denied the kind of possibility of productions that launched the generation of playwrights who still are perceived as the present generation – who are in fact the past generation.

These people being . . . ?

(*Laughs.*)

The responsibility is on theatres to choose the young playwrights that they believe are important and to back them and their work. That's what created the generation of playwrights who are seen as the major playwrights. My generation has had less of that kind of support. That's what's really created the current logjam. It's not that the amount of latent playwriting talent ever varies in a country. It remains constant. But what does alter is the opportunities of production, it's as simple as that.

An enormous amount has been done in the last ten or fifteen years to try to make the theatres more commercially practical, make them businesslike operations. Do you think that this has inculcated a set of priorities which it's very difficult to reconcile with artistic priorities?

I believe that it's made the job of running a theatre very difficult. It's created an incredible tension around the whole area of programming in which every play that's programmed is a big risk and a theatre doesn't have to accumulate very many failures before it has to close or the director has to resign. That obviously makes people reluctant to do new work that doesn't conform to pre-accepted notions. It also means that there's a temptation to double-guess the market, if you like, a temptation where an artistic director is setting out, hoping to meet an audience's expectation. Whereas I believe that if a medium is to move forward an artistic director should really be making a stand for what they consider to be aesthetically important and aspiring to extend the audience's expectations.

Personally I believe it's a matter of self-esteem, that it's a question of: are you simply going to accept your role as a part in a whole sequence of market forces, are you just another link in that chain, or do you have the right to your own voice and your own aesthetic and the right to stand for those? That's the choice that I've seen.

I think we can be thankful that there are people around who are producing work which is radically new, but they tend to be innovating from without. And to a certain extent this is what's always happened in the British theatre. It was only in rather exceptional circumstances, like the Royal Court in the fifties and sixties, that a theatre which belonged to the establishment was perceived as being at the forefront artistically. That created an expectation which these theatres can still fulfil with the odd production from time to time but they find it impossible to do so consistently.

What I see is that this generation, my contemporaries, are an exceptionally rigorous and imaginative bunch of artists. Those of us who have continued working and pursuing whatever ideals that we have are very tenacious. We've had to be realists. I've no doubt about the survival of this medium because of that. Perhaps simply we're experiencing a frustration because playwrights have to work with the existing theatrical establishment and so we been on the receiving end of these 'non-exceptional circumstances' as you call them.

I think one of the things which has caused a hangover effect with attitudes to new writing since the seventies is that the idea of Equal Opportunities was taken to an extreme. An idea arose that anyone could write at least one play based on their lives and so the less known, the less experienced the writer, the better in a way. I think playwriting is actually very hard. And not everyone can write a play which is rich enough to sustain actors and a director and a designer and an audience all participating in it. And I think there has been a great problem reconciling the quality of the work with equality of opportunity.

Certainly. It's a mixed legacy. There are real moral arguments for the work that's been done in the areas of racial, sexual and class politics, and I hope no one would deny that. At the same time the whole phenomenon of what's been labelled New Writing has been entirely ambivalent in terms of what it's achieved for playwriting. Because whereas in the past the new plays which were happening were assumed to be going on because they were the most exciting pieces of playwriting, now the playgoer may suspect that they may be going on because they're worthy New Writing. Good plays have been devalued by this context and consequently denied the audiences they deserve.

Do you feel aware that, as the world is becoming more multicultural and a smaller and smaller place and theatre is becoming increasingly internationalised, that the role of the writer is partly under threat because language is something specific to a particular group of people? That it's a shared means of communication which has a communal but also an isolating function?

The role of the writer becomes much more vivid in this situation because the specifics of each voice's qualities become more apparent. The possibility of a coexistence of an enormous range of voices within some kind of 'global culture' is an appealing notion. But I'm frequently disappointed that the spoken language of theatre can be bland and homogenised. The very nature of theatrical form requires certain things of language. It's required that language should be speakable and the choices of words be positive – and the shaping of the lines have a particular form that can be used by an actor, that can be delivered and that can have a kind of transparency, that can reveal aspects of the nature of the action that the speech is part of. I believe the whole question of the nature of language in drama is something that's mostly neglected in our theatre. And I think it's important to be positively aware of the nature of the language that you're using as you write and to give actors words that are tools that they can use powerfully. It isn't enough simply to create a drama and let the words be secondary to that.

In some ways this may be to do with the influence of televisual dialogue. There's a certain kind of speech that people now assume is the model of how people talk, as it were, normally. That flat tone is accepted as the idea of normality or reality but I think you only have to listen to anyone talking to realise that language is consistently complex and full of all kinds of forms and patterns. I suppose I'm just demanding that playwrights be perceptive to the possibilities that exist in the use of that.

How do you recognise good dialogue, do you think?

Such a profound question.

Is it something to do with listening? Because I'm always struck by the dialogue in your plays, that the characters listen very intently to each other, possibly more so than I as a typical member of the audience am likely to be doing at a given point.

This is an answer to a slightly different question, but I'm very aware how often I can sit down in the theatre and after the first five minutes I already know what's going to happen for the next two hours. I like the idea that an audience should not be able to do that, that a play should be really quite inexplicable although the sequence of events once they've happened should be retrospectively observed as entirely inevitable. Also I believe that the work should have a kind of density so that it requires an audience to listen hard. I really don't want an audience to sit back. I think that to use the medium well you need to keep people rapt.

So you think a playwright should actually be trying with the text **of a play to offer the audience an experience which could occupy all of their attention throughout the evening? The actual language of the play is what you hope the audience will spend their evening engaging with first and foremost?**

The best theatre is achieved when all the elements of performance coalesce, and the language is the central, the defining, element in that. I see my aim as primarily to propel the imagination of the audience. And I often think of it as trying to create a poem inside the audience's head. I calculate very finely what assumptions an audience may draw from what I'm presenting in front of them. I may show the audience a fragment, but a fragment that implies the existence of a whole – and I hope that the audience goes away with the whole.

matthew bourne
Adventures in Motion Pictures

Matthew Bourne is Artistic Director of Adventures in
Motion Pictures, a company he co-founded in 1987.
His choreography for AMP includes *Spitfire* (1988),
Deadly Serious (1992), *The Nutcracker* (1992), *Highland
Fling* (1994) and two films for television: *Late
Flowering Lust*, inspired by the poetry of John
Betjeman, and *Drip – A Love Story*, a contemporary
retelling of the Narcissus myth set in a Northern
theatrical boarding house.

When Adventures in Motion Pictures started out in '87, we were just graduates from the Laban Centre, which is a contemporary dance college in South East London. All that we knew then was that we wanted to work together and there just was no other work going. If you weren't actually going to get something off the ground yourself, then you would be doing nothing, probably.

Was it the workers seize the means of production or was it more a Norman Tebbit on-your-bike kind of operation?

I never think in those terms. I think it was more to do with the fact that we always wanted our own company, a few of us anyway, and we picked up some other people along the way. I could never see myself working for someone else, not as a dancer anyway. My talents as a dancer are very moulded by what I do for myself, so I can make myself look, you know, **good**. Because I create parts for myself I don't have to please anyone else.

Very early on, we did a piece called *Does Your Crimplene Go All Crusty When You Rub?* – heavy title! – which wasn't by me, it was by someone called Jacob Marley – his real name's John Heath. It was about old people in a sort of church hall, having a good time. And it was so different, this piece, that it just got the company noticed very quickly and we were asked to do some good one-offs at events that got us reviews. We'd only been going about three months and touring dates came in and things. We were responding to requests rather than trying to find things to do.

And were you playing old people?

Yeah. Sort of. We didn't have old makeup on and stuff . . .

But you were finding a new physical language . . .

Yeah. He has a funny style of movement peculiar to him. It's like grockles: grockles are non-dancers. So it didn't have a very dancy feel, it didn't have a technical edge to it . . . It was much more a **character** thing. It was something we very much enjoyed doing. Because at the college you were never asked to **be** anything . . . apart from yourself dancing. You get this funny thing: Am I supposed to be me in this piece or am I just this Body? It's a very confusing area. So this was something – character – we brought to it that was new.

From there I did a piece called *Spitfire*, which was based on a famous type of ballet, *pas de quatre*, which is normally done by ballerinas in white, romantic tutus, and I did it for men in white underwear. It was like a cross between a ballet and an underwear advertisement. You know the way they are in those catalogues: all sort of chummy, standing next to each other . . . Which is what got me noticed, got my career as a choreographer off the ground and found a way of doing pieces that I thought you could identify with, that had humour in them. The other main thing that we're known for now is pieces that have a humorous edge to them, an ironical sort of humour.

You seem to have a predilection for slightly old-fashioned arcadian situations which require a degree of heroic naivety . . .

Yeah. That's just me. I've always been a bit retro. Even when I was five I was retro. I've always loved the past, I've never been a very contemporary person, I must say. Sort of current music, things like that. I always look a lot **wider**.

What I really loved about *The Nutcracker* was that here was a classical ballet where the dancers on stage didn't behave like ballet dancers, they behaved like people. **And so they can push each other out of the way and sit on each other and get really pissed off . . . And you had found situations – where the dancers were playing scruffy kids in the orphanage or where they were trying to balance themselves on the ice – where dancing, which is perhaps in certain circumstances a slightly ridiculous activity, was viewed with a certain irony.**

I try and find movement that still works for the characters: and that's to do with **activities**, to do with situations where dancing is a natural thing. In the Betjeman film, because we were working with Nigel Hawthorne and a couple of other actors, who were not doing any kind of organised movement, everything that we did within the same scene had to stem out of reality and an activity. So there's a tennis dance, there's a golf dance, there's a swimming dance, there's an evening party dance, there's a sort of rave up where we dance all over the furniture where we're all a bit pissed: it all springs out of an activity. It's not like suddenly we all start dancing and it all slows down and it's like a Flake advert or something. It has to feel right.

Quite often they say: He's got quite limited steps, and all this kind of stuff. It's usually ballet fans or critics who are missing the big jumps and turns – as though they were relevant or **mean** anything. I'll put them in if I think that they'll add to it or they are relevant to something but I won't just put them in because people expect them. I want people to go with the story more than just looking for those steps, those tricks.

And you do manage a lot of very telling detail.

I get loads from ballet, I mean I'm not an anti-ballet person by any means. I used to go all the time. And I've learned most of what I know about organising people on a stage from ballet – not from contemporary dance but from classics.

I'm not really trained as a ballet dancer, so I've not got this great range of steps to call upon, I have to make them up, really – or use things from memory. I think if you're a ballet choreographer it's all there, it's just a case of what order you put it in. And how many times you repeat it.

But you do work with dancers who have quite a considerable amount of training?

They have to be . . . yeah, they have to be good.

Because that's what makes the difference between a laugh and genuine wit – the fact that they really can do the steps!

We are a dance company. And that's what we're funded as. And I don't want it ever to move away from that. That's what's different about us, I think.

Do you find it constraining at all to know: Well, we are funded as a dance company therefore we have to do . . .

No. Because I always approach everything from a dance point of view: is this relevant to dance? can it move? where's the idea coming from movementwise? I feel that what's good about the company is the communication through something that doesn't speak. I expect a lot from my performers, I suppose, in that they've got to be very good dancers as well as actors. And I feel that what we're working on, what we're developing, is something different, something quite original that no one else is doing.

I try and get the dancers to think like actors so that they'll say things like: This movement doesn't feel right for my character, or something like that, the sort of thing an actor would say. Usually dancers just do exactly what you tell them to. There's no question, the choreographer says do this and they'll do it. Which is silly really, they should have that input and then you get a more mature performance out of them.

Does humour have something to do with this? Certainly I know from working with actors, when you've got a good comic performance, a lot of that comes from the performer being the person who's got the timing and the delivery and the intuition to make that work. There's not some sort of directorial decision: (*clicks fingers*) Go there!

It's something you learn. Because you're not really taught to do it at dance college. You feel it eventually. And the people I've been working with for a while, we've learnt how to do that. And we've done a lot of shows together and they know what I want and they know there's a certain style of humour that we don't want. And some people will do it sometimes on stage and you have to stop them.

Give me an example.

Well, it's particularly difficult with the kids sometimes, in the orphanage scene, because we have to keep reminding ourselves that we're not trying to be kids, we're trying to be real people who happen to be kids. Because if you really **do** watch kids, you know, they're quite serious really, especially if they're orphans. To be funny, I think, you've got to be true, there's got to be a lot of truth in it. So you'll lose the humour if it's being thrown at the audience too much.

It seemed to work better and better in the _Nutcracker_ the nastier and more unpleasant the world became in which it was all happening.

Oh yeah. It almost makes you laugh at how horrible it can get, how awful these people can be. That can turn into humour. But if it's all too pantomimey and too obvious, an audience will react in the opposite way. My theory is that you can put a really obvious joke in if you play it completely straight and don't suggest it's funny at all. You just play it completely seriously and then it's funny. If you directed the audience to it in any way in your performance, they'd just think: God, that's pathetic!

You have to kind of let their imagination do part of the work. And it doesn't always have to be a very large leap . . .

Yeah. Don't always point to it. Let them **see** it . . . It's surprising what you can get away with if you turn something into a joke. Because we do this piece called _The Infernal Gallop_, a sort of French piece, all French clichés and stuff.

With subtitles?

Yeah. French dance with English subtitles. And we do this pissoir scene, it's just like a pick-up in a pissoir. Every time the men are about to **Do It**, they get interrupted by this band of street entertainers. They keep coming in and catching their . . . It's potentially very dodgy ground. Especially when you're touring – and in schools and things – because we actually go quite a long way with that, because we know it's just about to be broken with the joke. Just when people feel themselves starting to get offended, they laugh and it's all gone. It happens twice: they do it all again, and they come in again, and they get an even bigger laugh then.

I suppose there's always a gay element in what we do . . . Because we were originally uneven – four men and two women – if we go into duets, there's always two men together. And sometimes there's no explanation given for that. It's not an **issue** that that's happening. So in that sense it's a political thing, I suppose, as opposed to a humour thing.

I quite often have gay characters in our pieces or I'll subvert people's expectations of what the character is supposed to be. In the first half of *Deadly Serious* we do *Rebecca*, that's the basis of the plot. And I'm Max de Winter and I've brought Mrs de Winter back with me and we have this thing with Mrs Danvers and Mrs de Winter. But I'm also having an affair with Guy Haines from *Strangers on a Train* . . . It's funny because it's so **obvious** that it's happening but she doesn't notice, she's just this wimp who never notices anything. Now the audience find that funny. To a lot of the audiences we're going to, you know, they don't really see very much . . . you're introducing ideas to them that suddenly become more acceptable. And I've always found that humour is a good way of winning people over.

And are there particular directions which you want to follow with the company further into the future?

Nutcracker is the first large-scale piece that we've done and we're going to be doing another one. *Swan Lake*. That's a development: trying to make our style work on a larger group of people – something that's been quite intimate until now, which has required the audience to be quite close to us, to get involved in what we're doing at close range so that they can see the faces very clearly. And it's a different style of acting and you can do much more detailed, tiny movement that they can see. So that's all a challenge, a new thing for us.

The other thing I really want to develop is an audience that's not this audience of people who're frightened to come and see dance. There are a lot of people like that and they've been put off in the past by various things they've seen and what they tend to do is lump it all together as one thing.

But dancing is something so many people do and enjoy doing themselves. I would have thought, for that reason if for no other,

**people really ought to enjoy going out to see people doing it really
well. It's much more connected with what there is in a lot of kids'
daily lives than standing on a stage and acting.**

But the difference is it's something people are frightened of, you see.
Because they feel that they possibly don't understand it. So they don't trust
their reactions to it. You can go and see productions of *Swan Lake* which are
absolutely dreadful. And people go along and they think: Oh, well, it's a
masterpiece, isn't it? Yes, it was good, you know. And actually they didn't
like it at all, but they think they **should** like it. Quite often the response
you get from people when they come and see a show they have liked, it's a
relief that they understood it.

**I think dance is in a rather good position in that I think what
happened with opera in the eighties, where everyone sort of
suddenly discovered: Oh, here's a kind of theatre we can actually
like, is happening with dance and is likely to happen more.**

What other companies are you thinking about? Because I don't know that
that's true . . .

**I've seen some very enjoyable things recently. I liked Second Stride's
Escape at Sea—**

I liked that.

**—at The Place and the DV8 show *MSM*. And *Strange Fish*, which I
really enjoyed . . .**

Yes, they are very interesting, those shows. But they do have very limited
appeal, **really**. It's not this big boom. I think they're great, those shows, and
the Second Stride one I enjoyed very much but, you know, it was on for
three nights at The Place – you haven't even got a thousand people there.

**I knew for a fact that lots more people wanted to go than could
actually get tickets.**

Yeah, they were mad not to do more, but the thing is that it's getting beyond that cliquey, small audience that will always go and see those companies and finding something that's going to be an enjoyable night out for lots more people and not compromise and become bland and Wayne Sleep-ish. That's a new term: waynesleepish. Lovely man. Let's face it, you don't fill this place [Sadler's Wells] for two weeks if you're doing what Second Stride do, much as we all admire it and it does get a good audience. Unfortunately there isn't a big **enough** audience for it. And it's partly the educating of audiences in this country: they're not given the chance to see things and to get to like them enough.

If you go to New York and you see New York City Ballet, their repertory is three, four pieces a night. And the programmes change all the time – so you end up seeing things more than once. And there's an audience for that because it's been going on for years. Whereas here it's the same old things that are churned out again and again and people have got so used to seeing them . . .

Do you think there's any possibility of being able to create proper ballets now in the way that *Swan Lake* and *The Nutcracker* were created a hundred years ago?

You mean new ones?

Yeah.

Well, I think there is. It should probably be the next move, shouldn't it, after *Swan Lake*. The thing that draws me to doing a ballet like that is that for so many years now I've done pieces that have been based on an idea that I've had and had to get music from all over the place, lots of ideas. And they end up being quite collagey sort of pieces, almost like a revue, a series of sketches. And inevitably that's because of your score.

What attracts me is a written score of **great** music that was written to be danced to. And a **story** that's there already, that you can think: Well, what can we do with this? It's a really nice structure to start working on. And you've got all these preconceived conceptions of what it should be.

When we did the Hitchcock show, people all came with some idea, or some favourite bits of some favourite film, or something that they knew about him or the kind of work: they knew the world we were working in. Then you're halfway there. Because you can play with that then. So I think that probably would be the next move, to basically create something from scratch with a commissioned score. I think you could see from that *Nutcracker* that it's not alienating to anyone. It's a story you can follow. I don't like those great long programme notes that explain the story in a ballet. You don't **want** to tell everyone the story, anyway.

As soon as you give people programme notes they think that they're going to have to read it otherwise they're not going to understand. It's a cyclical process.

I think that's a good way to start: it's a good premise that no one has read anything in the programme and you're telling a story from when the curtain goes up. It's like Balanchine said, there are no mothers-in-law in ballet. I think that's right. He went completely in the other direction: there was no nothing in his ballets, just dancing. I think you can tell stories through a lot of means.

I think that, as well, is what these sort of theatres are crying out for. If you're going to do dance in big auditoria then it needs a form which addresses people on that scale.

Yeah, it's finding pieces that will appeal to a wide enough audience without, as I say, doing the most obvious things. That's why it's good doing *Nutcracker* and *Swan Lake*. Because they sell. Because they're **called** *Nutcracker* and *Swan Lake*. And it's not something you think: Ooh, make lots of money there – call it *Swan Lake* and give them something completely different . . . I want to get those people in and I don't want then for them to be disappointed. I want to deliver all the elements that they expect from those shows and all the magic and the kind of wonder of all those things. And I think there are ways of doing that now that are very much better than the tired old way that the *Nutcracker* in particular is being put across.

It's not actually very **good** for kids: a lot of it's really boring. All these girls who come with their mothers and go to dancing schools, you know;

who think it's all lovely to see the girls in tutus and on point and stuff. Fine, if that's what they're into. But for the average kid it's **not** very entertaining. There's nothing there to grab hold of, so that's why I tried in ours at least to give it a story. And they love watching the adults being kids and stuff and they get very involved and they look at it at a completely different level.

It's actually important to do this, I think, because otherwise the pieces will just dry up. It's **fantastic** music. It really needs a new approach. You know they all called it 'The Alternative *Nutcracker*' or 'The Anarchic *Nutcracker*'. It's **not** really. Because deep down it's true to what it was originally. And David Lloyd Jones, the conductor, agrees. He says Tchaikovsky would have loved it and he knows everything there is to know about him. So I'm quite happy about that.

I'm sure Tchaikovsky would have loved it as well.

Let's hope he likes the next one. That's going to be more daring in some ways, *Swan Lake*. It's a much more serious piece, it's a tragedy. The way I'm thinking of doing it as well could be quite controversial, I suppose.

katie mitchell
Keep working. Keep open.
Keep learning. Keep looking.

Katie Mitchell's productions for Classics on a
Shoestring include *Arden of Faversham*, *Vassa
Zheleznova*, *Women of Troy*, *The House of Bernarda
Alba* and *Live Like Pigs*. She has also directed *The Last
Ones* (Abbey Theatre, Dublin), *Rutherford and Son*
(Royal National Theatre) and four productions with the
Royal Shakespeare Company: *A Woman Killed with
Kindness*, *The Dybbuk*, *Ghosts* and *Henry VI: The
Battle for the Throne*.

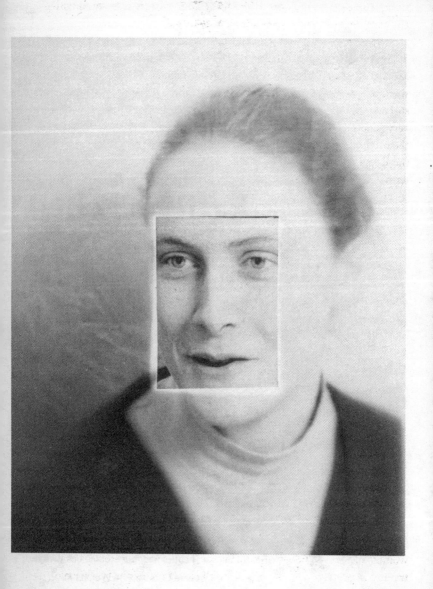

Do you enjoy working here at the RSC? You've been associated with the company for really quite a long time now.

When I started as an assistant it was tough – it would be dishonest of me to say that it wasn't. But it was a really good training: as much watching the work of a whole spectrum of different directors as it was to see how actors sustain work over a long period of time. The actors that I worked with were very generous and when I made mistakes, they were very open in correcting them. I was very lucky in that respect. And I suppose now, looking back on the directing work that I've done, the RSC has been incredibly brave in terms of the shows it's let me do: *A Woman Killed with Kindness*, which is described by most of the critics as completely unstageable because of the two sub-plots, *The Dybbuk* – imagine giving a goyim girl *The Dybbuk* to direct with a company of twenty-five actors, mostly male! and now *Henry VI Part iii*. So I feel deeply grateful.

Of course there are restrictions. You have to share actors and that's a difficult situation where you have to learn to make certain compromises. That can be tough. Also the actors can be very tired if you catch them late in the season when they've been performing for weeks on end and after the rehearsal day they're doing a performance every single evening.

Traditionally the RSC hasn't exactly been overflowing with women directors. Is there some special pressure as a result?

On me? I don't feel that, to be honest. When I first came it was a season where there were many, many women. There was Di Trevis, Cis Berry, Garry Hines, Deborah Warner, Sarah Pia Anderson . . . So it was a really strong and rich balance. Later I was critical of the imbalance of male to female directors. But I've subsequently discovered that it's not through want of trying on the RSC's behalf.

I'm passionate about ensuring that there are lots of female assistants coming into the company and of course passionate about having more women around as colleagues at many levels, not just as directors. I always try and make sure that the production team is predominantly female.

We had a fantastic time with *Ghosts*, where we had a female sound designer, female designer, female lighting designer – and we in fact did one of the swiftest techs in the history of the RSC. I don't know whether that was gender-specific or not, but we did it in a day! So I do like to work with women as colleagues but I don't feel under inordinate pressure because I'm a woman working in a predominately male environment. The main thing is to get the work right – and **better**. Sharp and clear and thrilling.

As well as doing a number of shows here you've also done a lot of work with your own company, Classics on a Shoestring. When you can work for the RSC—

Why do I go and work for no money? (*Laughs.*)

—what is there about Classics on a Shoestring, what does that give you that you can't find elsewhere?

It gives me total artistic control. Over casting. Over the conditions, the working conditions. Over the rehearsal room, the hours, all elements of staffing. So that's a very strong reason for still wanting to do it. Also I tend to do plays with Classics that no one else will let me do. Really dangerous choices that either aren't going to fit into the artistic programme or aren't going to bring bums on seats or whatever the prerequisites of any building I'm working for are.

And fundamentally I just like to test myself, to test my commitment. If you remove the issue of money and create a situation where— I mean I have to do all the fundraising for this as well, I have to work incredibly hard for no money over long periods of time – it's like having a check-up at the doctor: you know you are still doing it for absolutely the right reasons. It's like a touchstone, proving that one's not being seduced by success or money or whatever.

And does it have the same function for the other people who are involved?

In an ideal world it's not right that actors shouldn't be paid. And I don't think that that's particularly healthy. With the last show we managed to get ourselves in a position where we actually paid them quite a substantial fee for the performance period, although not for the rehearsal period.

As far as the people who work with me on the production side are concerned, I think that they do it for the sake of the work, for the love of the work and whether it's paid or not isn't really an issue.

They tend to be the people as well who you've worked with on your shows for the RSC . . .

They're the same team, completely, we all move *en masse.*

Do you think it's very tough if you're a freelance director, and somehow you can't get it together to run your own company, to have a career these days? To have a career in the sense of being able to . . .

Choose your own work.

. . . create and evolve a coherent aesthetic?

I think it's very difficult, incredibly difficult. In an ideal world, of course, one wants to do a sequence of specific shows in any one year. Sometimes there's only two or three of them. They are to do with a longer-term artistic development. But the freelance market will constantly manipulate, sour and sully that rich, clean line. And so you find you want to do one play and they'll say: Well you can't do that play, you can do a play which is **sort of** like that, by the same writer. And you find yourself in a cleft stick whereby you know that from an artistic point of view you have to do the former play but you're being asked to adjust . . .

So Classics on a Shoestring is a way to sidestep that . . .

For the greater artistic good. Yes. No one would let me do *Live Like Pigs* or *Women of Troy* or *Bernarda Alba* for a whole series of different reasons – *Bernarda Alba*, for example, because it had a huge hit in the West End, so no one wanted to touch it with a bargepole. But that's the joy of the company.

And you have to **work** as well, you really have to work. At every level, very hard. And when you come back into the RSC, you really respect the publicity department or the casting department or the front of house because you've actually done a lot of their work. So it's very good, it's a very good discipline.

But you don't want to do that all the time, you don't want to start a Grotowski-like community . . .

Oh well, that would be a dream! Of course. I mean always, always in the back of my mind is the thought that one should step out of the system as it stands and the values and the tastes of the theatre community and found one's own alternative way of working in very purist and almost monastic conditions. But that requires real balls. And also a very, very clear artistic vision. And I don't know whether anyone would fund it. Would somebody fund a two-year rehearsal process in a sort of converted chapel in the middle of South Wales? I don't know.

Well, Peter Brook managed to get funding for three years in 1970 from the Ford Foundation or whoever it was.

He did actually, didn't he?

It's just at the moment I think things like *Live Like Pigs* show what it's possible to do with theatre as a medium – and there are very exciting possibilities there – but at the same time theatre as an institution is in all sorts of trouble. What sort of effect do you think this situation, this difficulty, has on the acting profession?

Basically all actors want to work and they want to work hard and they want to do real work. I think the danger is that actors might be working with a series of directors who aren't challenging them at a very deep level, either artistically or politically. So they find themselves slightly ambushed when they do come across directors who do that. They're in the worst situation of all, actors, aren't they? I mean, they have so little power. I don't think that's particularly healthy. I think that one should find a situation whereby they're empowered more. And the only place at the moment where you can help is the rehearsal room, by creating more egalitarian working conditions.

Various actors have actually tried to set up companies and to do without a director . . .

I think that's a perfectly valid experiment. But the role of the director wasn't created by chance. It was created because there was a genuine need for an outside eye. Now, it's up to the individual director how they expand upon that basic tenet, but even if there are a group of actors working together without a director, I imagine that there will be one person who takes on that role, very quietly, very slyly perhaps, but one person will inevitably end up directing. But I'm not averse to that experiment, of course not.

I am conscious of people I know who are talented actors having great crises financially and also intellectually, of motivation, when they do hit a run of not working. Then, when they're in work they can't turn things down so they take on too many things in too short a space of time and end up completely knackered . . .

It's a real danger.

And I feel that that is bound to exact a price in terms of the overall standards in the profession. What I've seen of your work suggests that it really is all about how good the acting is. It's a type of theatre which it's impossible to do with people who aren't acting well. And I wondered what sort of perspective that gives you . . .

For me, when I'm casting, I respond about fifty per cent to the personality and about fifty per cent to the acting ability. I'm always looking for actors who interest me as people or who I feel are somehow **in charge** of themselves: they know who they are if you take away their role as an actor. And I think that creates a very specific type of acting.

Do you think acting is something that everyone can do?

I think it's a skill. It's something you can learn and work at, but basically you do need something – I don't know what it is – as a foundation. I don't quite subscribe to the theory that everyone can act. And I'm very wary of making generalisations about actors. Every actor is different and every actor has his or her own incredibly complex make-up and as a director you're trying to decode and enable and release and focus all the things which make up each individual actor. It's so specific . . .

One of the things that impressed me about *Live Like Pigs* was the ability that the actors had to sustain a situation and an intensity over an extended period. Acting was visible there as a team sport rather than some sort of expression of rampant individualism.

A lot of the credit is due to those actors who were without doubt an extraordinary group of individuals **before** you look at them as actors. And the main thrust of those rehearsals, as with most rehearsals, was to get the ensemble to commit to the bigger idea, of what the play's really about, and then to work on the detail of it. Early on in rehearsals no one plays their own part, for at least two weeks, so that they're constantly being asked to commit to the work beyond the limits of their own character.

But they know in advance which character they're going to play?

Of course. I wouldn't have a running audition situation. That would be disastrous.

With Classics on a Shoestring, you have been able to work with a number of actors more than once—

Which is great, really great!

Is this a resident company, as it were?

Well, there are a few people who do work regularly with Classics but most of the casts are effectively new companies, cast specifically for the piece in mind with the hope that they will gel as an ensemble of people and be able to work together. When casting I try to avoid bringing a group of people together who aren't going to get on – if that happens then rehearsals can start to become about why certain egos do not get on in the room, rather than the work in hand. And that's exhausting, time-consuming and not very constructive. So casting is the most difficult area, really.

Is there anything you can think of to say to any actors who might be reading this?

Don't despair. Keep working. Keep open. Keep learning. Keep looking.

Do you have another production in prospect for Classics on a Shoestring?

Yes, we do. We're sort of working out **what** at the moment. We were going to do the Mystery Plays. It's quite an undertaking, though. The reason that we put the project on the shelf was because we realised that all of us, lighting designer, designer, dramaturg, musical director, movement director . . . we needed to spend at least a year preparing it. It's a mega-epic – and there are so many decisions to be made: do you do it in the original, do you update it like Tony Harrison, what do you do with it? We felt that we were rushing into it. We will definitely do it at some stage, but not in the near future.

At the moment I'm very interested in civil war, so I should imagine that the likelihood of it being a civil war piece will be high. The joy of Classics on a Shoestring is that it can respond swiftly. A decision can be made to do a text four weeks, say, before we start rehearsals. My great fear about the company is that we start to plan so far ahead that we can't actually respond to anything that's happening. If the civil war ended in former Yugoslavia and an equivalently apocalyptic event happened elsewhere and one wanted to respond, one could do that with Classics. So what I'm saying is: I don't know what the next play will be, but – probably at the end of this year, and, if not, at the beginning of next year – a crazy project will be launched and some extraordinary actors will yet again agree to leap into the breach.

Is there a problem – which applies to all theatre to a certain extent – that when you address a contemporary issue, the people who you really want to see that are the ones who don't come? The people fighting in Bosnia will not be able to see *Henry VI Part iii*, for example. Is there a certain limitation there to what one can achieve?

Let me be clear about this production, so we're not talking generally. I actually went to former Yugoslavia in the summer because I wanted to find out first-hand what was happening there. I also felt a strong moral responsibility to respond, be that working for the Red Cross, Amnesty International, or directing a theatre production there or here. And the thing that struck me most of all was that my skills are directing so it would be insane for me to train as a nurse or do something like that. So I tried to find a play that was about civil war here. Because I thought it would be worth reminding people that this isn't an isolated event that happens in other countries, it has happened on our own turf. And by analysing how it happened, why it happened and who it happened to **in Britain**, perhaps that would enable the British audience to put a different pair of glasses on when looking at the situation in former Yugoslavia. So the production is aimed specifically at a British audience. Does that make sense? It's to help us come to some sort of broader understanding of the situation. So it isn't actually designed for the Bosnian audience.

Sure. I'm not really suggesting that it is.

If you're wanting to reach people, beyond a certain type of regular theatre audience, then you have to lower the seat prices – I think that's the first thing you have to do – and the whole formality and the ritual of visiting theatre needs to be made less daunting. For example, if I go to a football match I don't know what the rules of the ritual are, I don't know how I buy a ticket, I don't know how I go in, which gate I go in, which gate I come out of, and it must be the same for someone who, say, goes to football matches regularly when he or she approaches the Barbican or any theatre: what are the rules? what do you wear? all of those sort of things . . .

It's normally a bit easier to find a football ground than it is the Barbican.

(*Laughs.*) There is that, yes. But I think you have to address all those external areas first.

I was asking more because I think the idea of doing a theatrical performance in order to prevent people doing a particular thing or to encourage them to do a particular thing is really rather simplistic and it's not going to work. So what exactly is the sphere of influence which it's possible to move in? Are we restricted to an expression of grief at what's going on?

The production will only pose a question: What is our responsibility in the face of civil war in another country? What we now need to do is to stop being forced to respond to the immediate violence and pain and upset of what's happening in former Yugoslavia and try and see it in a much broader moral, ethical and historical context. And I suppose that's really what I'll be gently doing with the production, trying to open up the debate from a different angle.

At the centre of the play is a king who has a very strong moral, ethical and spiritual sense of himself and the world in which he's living. He's surrounded by people whose obsessions are power and ambition. And of course the two forces clash in the play. I think that's an interesting conflict. But ultimately I want people to come and see the work and judge for themselves.

stephen daldry
There is a new audience out there

Stephen Daldry currently holds 'Best Director' awards both in London and on Broadway. He was Artistic Director of the Gate Theatre, Notting Hill, from 1989 to 1992 and is now Artistic Director of the Royal Court Theatre. His recent productions include *Pioneers in Ingolstadt*, *Purgatory in Ingolstadt* (both with Annie Castledine) and *Damned for Despair* at the Gate, *An Inspector Calls* and *Machinal* for the Royal National Theatre and *Search and Destroy* and *The Kitchen* at the Royal Court.

A lot has been made of your productions transporting large plays into the tiny atmosphere of the Gate or ripping *An Inspector Calls* out of a traditional theatrical vocabulary and transplanting it to a new one, or drawing *The Kitchen* out of the proscenium into an environmental piece. No one could have gone along and thought these productions had just simply happened like that, they're all shows which reveal a conscious directorial decision behind them. How important is that to you – to produce a reading of the play?

It's not a reading. It's creating a world. In *The Kitchen* you need to create a kitchen. And you need to create a kitchen where there is a specific service that is circular in motion as defined by the playwright. He'd written this thing with a circular service in it, therefore it seemed only natural that you had to realise the circularity of that central metaphor. You could have shoved it onto an end stage but it would mean squeezing it into a proscenium, so it's better to reveal the play for what it actually is.

Machinal had very specific things, it was defined again by the playwright, what she felt the world should be like. It is an interpretation but an interpretation of what her desires were. Her desires were pretty specific, it isn't moving away from those. And then you always have to take on board the space which you're producing in because that's the world as well. You can't pretend that the world is only behind the proscenium: the world is the whole space, including what the audience sit on as well.

On *An Inspector Calls*, the basis of that was that he had **not** written a play that was based on the world of 1930s' English drawing-room thrillers, but that was the original director in this country, Basil Dean's, interpretation. So most of the time the intention is to release the text from the original directors, and to try in some way to get back to the author's intentions. That was certainly the case on Priestley.

I thought it was very interesting, that show, because a lot of people's reactions to it were stylistic, they were responding to the aesthetic of it – whereas what interested me was what it was saying about Britain as a country.

I agree with you, yes, I couldn't agree with you more.

Does this sort of reception irritate you?

Well, in a way it does. It's only because some people are so aesthetically and visually and theatrically moribund and retarded in this country, people tend to have a peculiar and childlike attitude which can be joyous on one hand but irritating on another. You want them to grow up so that they can actually talk intelligently about what they're seeing but they can't yet. There isn't a vocabulary in which to talk about the visuality of theatre.

So what can someone in your position do to try and make them grow up? Is there anything you can do?

No. Very little. You just carry on doing work. I don't mean to be as rude really as I've just been but it just goes back to the simple basic notion that we come from a text-based root.

In a way I'm very surprised – and pleasantly so – at the success which *An Inspector Calls* has had. I was very excited when I saw it and thought this was a kind of theatre which I think had been waiting to happen for some time: where a director would take a very free approach to what seemed a traditional English play and by doing that unlock the meaning of it and make it more immediate. But in a way I think the success of it in the West End has actually proved what Priestley was complaining about, the fact that the British somehow have a tremendous capacity to ignore their own social problems.

What's interesting is that it **is** a success in the West End. A cyclorama and a little bit of scenery isn't going to make people want to come to the theatre. And the fact that the play itself is still resonant for that audience is fantastic and quite extraordinary, really, that such an upfront, political piece of basically agit-prop theatre can survive in the West End. It was written for the 1945 election to make people vote Labour, that was its intent, and people are still going along to see why they should vote Labour. And there is a sort of romanticism in the piece and people I think respond to that.

Schiller called the theatre 'the moral institution'. Do you feel that it has this moral function?

It can have. People talk about that, don't they? They talk about that particularly here at the Royal Court. I always resist it as much as I can when people say it should have that. I don't think the theatre **should** be anything to anyone, because as soon as you put a 'should' in front of any art form it immediately kills it. Having said that – here's the rider! – I think theatre is a perfect house, much better than cinema, in which to talk about moral values because it exists upon a dialogue and therefore the dialogue between the actors and the audience and between the audience themselves is undoubtedly— it's a public debating chamber. What's interesting about the theatre now is people still get more offended at watching real people fucking, nudity or violence on stage than people ever will watching a funny little box in the corner of the room or even on celluloid, so it is a more immediate form of expression.

Is morality just one of many agendas within the theatre? What are the reasons that you're doing it for?

Well, there is no obligation, again it goes back to the 'should', there's no obligation to do anything. My particular agenda happens to be a political one, you know, that's just me. I tend to veer towards public plays. I point that out out of interest, rather than it's something I tend to look for when I'm reading a play. It's interesting that's where they tend to fall – and ones that tend to be either rooted in or written out of a political or moral impulse.

Shall we talk about the Royal Court? Are you conscious of pursuing a particular aesthetic line here? Are you thinking when putting the programme together of wanting to show people that the theatre can have a particular nature that it doesn't have in other theatres in this country?

The Royal Court was created with a variety of different intentions by old George Devine and a lot of those intentions have been lost over the years.

One of them was to create a house which was as much an actors' and a designers' and a directors' house as much as it was a writers' house. It's become more focussed on writers in the last ten years with a not-conscious directorial aesthetic that's been placed upon new writing, which is as dominant as any other directorial imposition. The plays tend to be done within this poor man's aesthetic, an aesthetic which is absolutely rigid, not only in the Royal Court, but also in other theatres where new writing has cropped up.

You mean the kind of specious naturalism with real furniture and a lot of props and scene changes **where funny little people wearing black come on and move everything around to the sound of someone's favourite record while pretending that the audience doesn't know they're there?**

The form is outmoded, outdated and of no relevance and it has not challenged the writers. I mean, why and how we could be in a position where directors say new writing is too much like television when it's the directors who've imposed the aesthetic of television on new writing seems to be appalling.

So that's one of the agendas: to say new writing is not going to be . . .

The most boring experience you've ever had in a theatre.

. . . and could have had on television. This is not the writers' fault. The writers haven't been writing plays for television. It's just that the directors are taught to be dominant in their aesthetic. We need to change that.

There are other agendas and the Royal Court should be about new **work**, not just about new writing. And new work is a broad idea, we can involve everything from performance art to new interpretations as much as anything else. It seems to me that theatre has always fallen down where it's tried to impose a formula on the creative impulse. Because the creative impulse is bound to be and should be as variant and as wild as the artist or artistes wish to make it; you cannot create a dominant aesthetic within a building. No, it's got to be freer than that. It should be freer than that. This is not me, this is George Devine! You can't have an artistic policy, your artistic policy is who you ask to come into the theatre: that's your artistic policy.

And your artistic policy thus far is to have as wide and divergent a range of people and styles . . .

As possible. And it's also not to jump a process, one has to do that and it takes a long time, one has to start feeling around and know who's doing what and listen to the gutter as well as to the stars.

What are the vibrations that you're getting about what's going on in the British theatre at the moment? Do you think it's an interesting time?

Yeah, it's a fascinating time. It's a fascinating time. I mean we're having a huge burst of people wanting to see new work and new work being delivered and that's exciting.

Do you feel that the Royal Court is in a rather invidious position because so many people have expectations of it?

Yeah, I mean that's just a real bore but you've just got constantly to try and ditch and try and ignore. Which I'm getting better at.

Is the problem because other theatres aren't keeping their end up?

No. No. That's not true, there are other theatres that are buzzing, in the regions as well as in London. That isn't the problem. I think the problem really is that the Royal Court has always had a reputation for being a dissident theatre, which is fine and has been fine for many years, especially when there has been a coherence, an ideological coherence behind that dissidence. And when that's collapsed, it's difficult to see how it can work as a dissident theatre any more, really.

Is it a problem trying to be a dissident theatre in Sloane Square?

'Twas always thus.

Do you think some people take this theatre too seriously?

Oh, some people, yes. Of course. It changed the shape of British theatre once and they constantly want it to do the same. George Devine and the English Stage Company were lucky to be a certain age at a certain point with certain aspirations, which by luck happened to coincide with a point at which British society was changing. British society is in regression. If anything is going to happen in the theatre, theatre can only expand as the society itself wishes to expand. It is only a reflection of that society. If the society is moribund, the theatre can't do very much to combat that. It certainly can't lead any change within aesthetics or politics.

On the other hand particular people can use the theatre as a vehicle to contribute something to society which would not otherwise be there.

Yeah, sure. But the great theatre companies and the great moments in theatre worldwide have happened not just because there was a great individual but also because the society's been at the point where it needs a great individual to happen.

How much, though, do you think the theatre is dependent on individuals and how much on groups? As a director very often the reviews of shows you've been involved in have concentrated very firmly on your contribution. Do you feel that sometimes people attribute all sorts of powers to directors which they don't actually have?

In my case particularly. I tend to work very collaboratively. The only thing I think I do is try and create a context in which people can do something wild. The people I work with all the time, Rick Fisher, Stephen Warbeck and Ian MacNeil, we all know that linkage between us. It's quite difficult, for example, to tell the actors that they can take notes from Rick Fisher, the lighting designer, or Stephen Warbeck. Some people find that odd, but it's running with wherever the ball is and allowing the field to be open for the ball to be run with. Again that seems to be the proper role of the director really, to take anything from anywhere if it's of any use. If somebody's motoring, then clear the motorway and let them go. And that's as true of directing a play as it's true of running a theatre.

Having pursued this model of the motorway – if there is a crash, presumably you're the person who gets blamed. Are you afraid of failing?

I'm getting much more cavalier about it actually. I mean, again it's about confidence, isn't it, but it's also about people's pressure and aspiration for you being less important, and that your own internal aspirations become more important. And it's about career becoming less important as you grow older. It seems more important to do what you fancy doing rather than: it would be really fantastically **useful** to do *Tristan und Isolde* in Greece National Opera right now – or whatever. You can't do shows because they're career choices.

To look aside from your own work, are there particular things which you would like to see happen in the British theatre over the next few years? Do you have ambitions that are more formulated for the art form as a whole or for the Royal Court?

One of the things I've been trying to do is plug into the experiment in form, in the language in which we speak in theatre, the theatrical language, which went through a huge period of experimentation in the late eighties. A lot of it was rooted in Ruth Berghaus, spending a lot of time in Frankfurt . . .

And through a realisation that the content and the presentation didn't have to be identical.

Also finding that there were experiments in form, and people being interested not necessarily in the content, that the content was only a means by which the form could be expressed better. And I think that the journey of the last few years has been trying to marry that form and content so the aesthetic movement has become something of a redundant movement now.

I think that's the major task lying ahead of the British theatre at the moment: somehow to take the interesting possibilities which have been thrown up by a generation of directors exploring new theatrical vocabularies and apply these to new plays.

And reintegrating them with what people want to talk about. I couldn't agree with you more. That's what the Royal Court should be doing, it should have the tools of questioning the vocabulary of the theatre, but it should also be encouraging people to write knowing or having no limits to what they can or how they can write. There has been a rejection by some of the younger writers to tackle larger themes, and so there tends to be a pull towards quieter, more introverted pieces about families, family drama, which is, as far as I can understand it from an American model, a reactionary movement because it's about a movement away from public plays into private plays.

People argue very strongly that this is the New Writing proper, which I'm sure it is, but I would prefer to see plays moving back more into the public arena because I think it is a form that lends itself, as we were saying earlier, to the public debating arena. And whilst private plays can be incredibly powerful, the resonance of the best of them comes from their reflections on a wider, public morality.

And also we've talked about the problems of maintaining a diverse audience, not just people who live in Sloane Square . . .

The traditional London audience is what, two hundred thousand people who go – whatever it is – once or twice a month to the theatre. That base audience that the West End has been relying on – and the Royal Court to some extent – for many years is in decline. So in a sense one is seeking a new audience. But the new audiences do not want to see the plays that the base audience want to see.

Well, this has caused a huge consternation amongst West End producers because they only know what that two hundred thousand people will want to see: a Noël Coward or an Alan Ayckbourn. When the base audience goes, and actually the West End audience isn't wanting to go and see an Alan Ayckbourn, you suddenly realise Alan Ayckbourn has to move back into the subsidised sector. And they don't know what the **fuck** to do then. Which is why we need new producers in the West End as well. So everybody's bemoaning the end of an audience. Yes, it's true, there is an end of a traditional audience. That's OK, that's a good thing. There is another audience out there. And the other audience is much more resilient than the old audience. And we've found that even here. And it's interesting going back to the notion of the Royal Court being a dissident theatre. The dissidents tend now to be different. And one can put on a play by Sarah Daniels, it's hammered by the critics, it does fantastic business.

Well, it was a very good play!

I'm glad you said that.

It was.

Somehow you can get beyond what the critics say. And that's also true of plays like DV8 or Neil Bartlett investigating why his father used to go and watch puff shows in the 1950s and what on earth that was all about – and he gets an audience, I think that's fascinating, really. I mean it's a very different audience than would normally come to the Royal Court.

Is there a certain agenda in exploring male sexuality?

It's about running with the ball. You could argue – and some people do – that the gay rights movement in this country or in America is the civil rights movement of our generation. Therefore it is the dissident movement of our generation. In this sort of theatre, you have to reflect where that dissidence comes from: were it to be coming from the Greek Cypriot audience, no doubt we'd be doing a lot of Greek Cypriot plays. At the moment it happens to be coming from the gay writers, so we're doing gay plays. In the eighties there was a lot of movement in women's writing and we did women's writing.

In that sense you're not being proactive. You can't decide: I think we should do lots of gay plays. You can only say: This is a movement in society that we have to be engaged with. You may not even be arguing politically – you may be arguing for your own fucking financial survival because that's what people want to come and see!

As it happens, you've got a series of artists working within that field that are vocalising the aspirations, hopes or anger of a sizeable part of the population and they are married: the population that want to see it and the writers that are writing it. It doesn't always happen like that, you can get a situation where the Greek Cypriots are very angry and there's nobody writing.

Are you aware of plays having to be about something, an issue that can be encapsulated in three lines of leaflet copy?

Not at all. No.

Because from the consumer side of things it can sometimes seem that many plays that go on seem to have a neatly-formed thematic conundrum.

I would say that most of the plays that go on aren't like that and the exceptions are plays like that. The David Hare trilogy is an exception. But then you could argue that one of the great things about American writing at the moment is that the writing is so public and that's what's capturing people. We weren't that interested in plays about dysfunctional families coming from America in the seventies; now suddenly we're getting plays like *Oleanna* or *Angels in America* and people are fascinated. And those are big, popular plays with large public issues. People want to engage issues on that level, rather than why their father didn't love them as a child. Which I think can only be a good thing. And in a sense I would like the English plays to be more public, that tends to be what I'm excited about.

And do you see ones which are doing that? Have you got things coming up in the pipeline here that you're excited about?

Yes, of course. We have about thirty writers under commission, so it's difficult to talk about any individual. There are many writers that are writing in that arena, yeah. And some that obviously aren't. That's fine, too.

Have you got any plans to do a new play by a British writer?

You must be joking! (*Laughs.*) No, of course. I'm going to do a play by James Stock. What else am I going to be doing? That's the only one I've got definitely booked in for myself.

Is that *Star-Gazy Pie and Sauerkraut*?

Have you read it?

Yeah. Quiet weird. I'm not quite sure I understood what it was about. That definitely is not a play you can sum up in four lines of leaflet copy, to be absolutely fair.

No indeed. That's a big play. Big plays is what we want.

More bigger plays now!

More bigger plays now!

Is doing *The Kitchen* in a way a sort of gesture of throwing down the gauntlet to those writers and saying . . .

Only in a little way. It's not meant to be confrontational, it's more about saying that you can do anything. I mean it's difficult to do *The Kitchen* and it obviously makes no sense to do *The Kitchen*. And that's good.

I think for far too long we've been living in this country where everything's got to make sense, that people aren't reaching for what's impossible, they're only reaching for what they believe or understand or have been told what the possibilities or the limits are. And that's true on *The Kitchen*. You suddenly come and say: Well, we want to do this play and it's ridiculously expensive and we can't afford twenty-eight actors . . . Let's find a way of doing it. So you lead with your artistic nose rather than any of your financial noses.

The danger is that our ambitions have not been intent on searching out the extraordinary but only to compromise all of the time with the ordinary. And the problem with compromising with the ordinary is that it kills the nature of theatre, but also the nature of the audience that you're trying to build up. People **want** the extraordinary and it's only through giving them the extraordinary, allowing the audiences to support that, that you will ever declare to an Arts Council or to a Government that you can **do** the extraordinary.

And I think it's true of funding in this country that people want to fund ambition. There's no point in saying to the Arts Council: Look, we'd like to do a play with twenty-eight people, will you give us an increase of £60,000 in your budget? They'll say no. If you start doing plays with that many people in and: Now we want to carry on doing this, we need more money, then your argument is inevitably bound to be much stronger.

That's a way as well of trying to broaden the audience.

Of course, that's the only way of broadening the audience. And it's a weird, strange, old-fashioned, morality at work that says you cannot, you should not spend this money, you should not have that aspiration. It isn't dependent on the amount of money or what the aspiration is.

There is this notion – it comes from Government as well – about spendthrift artists. One is not being a spendthrist artist, one is creating endeavours which are rooted in very fixed and coherent budgeting systems.

But it's allowing those budgetary systems to be flexible and fluid to allow the aspiration of the artist to be realised.

At the same time as they're concerned about you spending lots of money, people are also concerned about you not paying actors.

That's what we're spending the money on: actors. The *Kitchen* set is not a particularly expensive set at all. And we have more actors here than we've ever had on the Royal Court stage since 1960-whatever. Yes, there are seventeen, eighteen actors paid on stage. It is an appalling draw on our resources. Yes, we went to Equity and said: To make up the waitresses can we use people from the YPT or people who've just come out of drama school as an educational experience? Yes, Equity said. In a sense it's not about **not** paying actors, it's about paying **more** actors than we've ever paid before and actually allowing other people to come in to realise the piece.

And of course people get upset about that and in a sense quite rightly: it should be that we can pay twenty-eight actors on stage at the Royal Court, now it just so happens that we can't. We can pay more than we could ever pay before because *Oleanna*'s a success in the West End. But to not do a show because you can't afford it . . . It's the same philosophy that we used to have at the Gate. We could, with the money we were making at the Gate, have done two-handers and paid Equity minimum. We could not have done Tirso de Molina and that Spanish Golden Age season. It seems to me it would be giving up the ghost to do that.

I think there are powerful arguments to ask people to work unpaid when it's still something exceptional. It is different when you start running a theatre as an institution where that becomes a system.

Oh, you can't have a theatre on that sort of basis, no. That would be appalling. You can run a theatre on a system – again like the Gate – where everyone is paid the same and the more money that comes in, then everybody gets paid more.

It is a serious problem for me and it does go back to this situation where if you're not willing to try the impossible, then I'm not sure why one would want to do the job. What tends to happen now is that if I read a play and I know how to do it, then chances are I'll give it to someone else, because there's no point in me doing it. And so one is constantly trying to look for the piece where one has no idea how on earth one would do it.

I remember once you described choosing whether or not to direct a play as being like deciding whether you're going to fuck somebody or not.

Yes, indeed. And one becomes less promiscuous as time goes on.

You seem to have been sleeping with some very strange people recently: Arnold Wesker and Sophie Treadwell . . .

No, not at all, Arnold's well worth fucking.

. . . while maintaining a long association with J.B. Priestley.

Yes, always getting back into bed with that old corpse. But no, that's true. Because it is a process of falling in love with something. And not knowing where that relationship will go.

Do you spend a lot of time thinking about doing a production before you actually decide: Yes, it's got to be this play.

What tends to happen, literally the process is: I read a play and decide whether I want to do it straight away. I usually read it and then go: Yes, I think this is fantastic. Then I usually spend a number of months working out whether I really do think it's fantastic without going back to the play; and then go back to the play after a period of a number of months and then read it again.

I try and read the play as few times as I can get away with before I go into rehearsal, which means it's difficult to design for. Which is why one prefers to design after – which is what we did on *Machinal*, not design it, just design the empty space and do the rest of it once we were in rehearsal. Because you want to make sure all you're responding to basically is a text and you don't want to get a production in your head before you go into rehearsals.

But you have to cast it.

Which is difficult. Essentially, all you really want to do is get your favourite actors together and cast them a couple of weeks in, which nobody wants to do these days: they want to know what they're playing. That would be the best way of doing it but nobody will let you do it. Did Peter Stein ever do that?

Yes, but they used to have huge fights.

Sounds great!

neil wallace
Inspiring change

Neil Wallace has been programme director of Tramway
in Glasgow since it became a permanent venue in
1991. He was previously Deputy Director of Festivals
for the City of Glasgow and as such was responsible
for the building's conversion into a performance space
to house the only British performances of Peter
Brook's *Mahabharata* in 1988 and a variety of special
projects for Glasgow European City of Culture in 1990.

At Tramway we're active in two main fields of work. One is extremely easy to identify: visual arts. What was once a big foyer space is now a space dedicated to exhibitions and the visual arts. We originate all our own shows. The second strand is partly easy to describe in that it's performance, the performing arts, but less easy to define because it has to deal with highly innovative, really quite progressive, unusual work which is of interest to us from abroad and which we want to support within the British Isles. So within the performance field, quite literally anything is possible.

We have no resident company but we do have, shall we say, informal associations with artists and companies. We have a number of groups and directors and artists who are associate companies – at least in our terms. Now I suppose the obvious one of those is Brook – he'd probably laugh if he heard me say he's an associate artist at the Tramway – nonetheless, he was the *raison d'être* of the space and he has recently presented the fifth of his productions to be seen in Glasgow.

We also have a link with other fairly well-known names in the international field. Robert Lepage is a director with whom we've worked a lot in Tramway, the Wooster Group from New York, Lev Dodin's Maly Drama Theatre, the Wrestling School . . . We have more loosely-formed associations with companies like Gloria, Siobhan Davies, Anne Teresa de Keersmaeker, Deborah Warner – a very important artist for us – and typically some of the most interesting work in Scotland: Communicado, Boilerhouse, Clanjamfrie, the young artist Ken Davidson . . . people whose names will be less known to audiences south of the border or further afield.

The fabric of a good Tramway season is a vague promise to the public that they will be seeing these artists in the near future – so it gives people a warm feeling that they can reacquaint themselves with work of absolutely the highest standard. It's nearly always innovative, sometimes innovative to the point of being mesmerisingly difficult. And that's how the pattern works – I don't know what happens between that and us putting together a piece of print because a lot of it is to do with the kind of aleatorism of how things happen and are put together: intuition, the offers that are made, the things one sees, the ideas that other colleagues in Britain or further afield have.

But somehow, despite the difficulty in this rather eclectic approach, you've managed to make a creative virtue out of being . . .

Unpredictable.

. . . a theatre which does not originate its own productions.

Oh absolutely, I think we're unusual on our **scale** in Great Britain but we're not unusual in concept. There are spaces in London that one would never dream of categorising as theatres: the ICA, Riverside, The Place Theatre – which even though it's a dance venue takes a very broad view of the performing arts . . . The nearest models really are in France, the network of the *maisons de la culture*, of which the big ones are on the periphery in Paris: Bobigny, Créteil, these kinds of places. These are the paradigms of this model, working at a much more developed level because they have ten times the funds.

I think in recent years the British theatre as a whole has perceived the virtues of co-productions and the need to see a good production in as many places as possible.

Yes, but I'm not interested in co-productions in order to save money – it's a collective response to a thrilling artistic idea or risk. It is an important point, because a broader part of our brief is an obsession about **sharing** things, about distribution. We have a kind of gateway function in Britain. Tramway is lucky in that it can somehow afford or find the resources to bring quite major work which then goes away again – something which is contrary to my nature.

And it's an exciting time to be working in this field here because something has been happening over the last handful of years. A group of theatres with slightly more traditional ideas of themselves as repertory theatres have become interested in a new kind of diversity in programme. And what these theatres have also begun to realise is that the process of forming a consortium, of acting, thinking, programming and taking risks as a member of a consortium, is a tremendously strengthening and stimulating exercise.

It's strong for the work because it means that an artist like – it hasn't yet happened in Britain but I hope it will – Deborah Warner ought to be produced by a handful of theatres in Great Britain and presented in a space which is suitable for her. For example, a theatre like Nottingham Playhouse might well be desperate to co-produce a Deborah Warner piece, to put real money into the production, to present the work, but they would either be faced with the task of doing major alterations to the Playhouse in order to achieve the environment she wants, or finding a space within the city where they could present it properly.

A handful of years ago you couldn't have imagined such possibilities would even be discussed among such a group of theatres and now they are. I think this is an unmarked but rather important contribution to the theatre life of the country because it means that work which might originally only have been seen at the Edinburgh Festival or in Avignon and the great cultural centres of the world can now not only be seen **in** Britain but can be distributed **throughout** Britain. Peter Brook is making his first ever genuine tour of the British Isles with *The Man Who*. To have talked this over just a few years ago would have been a joke, a waste of breath, but he is **doing** it.

Just recently you've done a whole series of Romanian productions.

This is a very important example of the process by which partnerships can be created in the name of a single idea, in this case rather an exotic idea, possibly a rather idiotic idea. The proposition was: Are there grounds for a long-term exchange programme between the British and Romanian theatre communities? Answer: Let's find out by taking ten people out to Romania for a festival and see what they think. And of course back they all came and the result of that was an admittedly young but quite energetic network: maybe a dozen people being extremely stimulated by the work that they'd seen there, the people they'd met, the possibilities for exchange, and who are just getting on and doing it.

It's not just a question of touring, it's a question of getting involved in creative workshop, co-productions, training workshops over there, their directors coming to work and run workshops here, management place-ments, seasons of British work in Romania and so on.

This too is a part of the whole – I don't know whether to call it an aesthetic or an ethic, I find it a moral thing – about getting more and more people involved in these kinds of projects. Because in the end it **inspires change**. In the end it's about casting light on the home practice: on whether what is happening in your theatre is relevant and whether there are alternative ways of producing the work and so on. All these things are catalytic.

Financial problems aside, there is a lot more foreign theatre available now in this country than there was ten years ago.

There's been a minor revolution. I can remember when I first had this bee in my bonnet. I was a Regional Arts Association officer in the early eighties and the most imaginative, inspiring international exchange was going on in a number of oases: Cardiff, London International Festival of Theatre, Riverside Studios as it then was, the Traverse doing a little bit, and the Edinburgh Festival – and that was it. Good night. Everything else was a bonus.

Now more and more British theatre organisations are exploring and making contact with colleagues in Europe, and that's very exciting. There's been a complete sea change in under fifteen years. And I think the big breakthrough has been made by people traditionally running the larger theatres, the reps and so on. The Lyric was always a shining example, inviting foreign directors to work with British companies. I think the sheer professional curiosity about what is happening abroad in the repertory theatre field is very important.

At Tramway the sort of set-up that you've got allows artists, the people who are actually creating theatre pieces, to spend their time doing that and not administering the building and worrying about fire regulations or who's selling the ice creams. But is there a downside to that as well, where you feel you're not really in control of what you're presenting and you're reliant on shopping?

No. I don't think so. This is a complicated question. There are downsides to that particular building because it's a very difficult space: technically it's not overstaffed, it's not terribly well provided for for artists' facilities – to come in and work there can be a very primitive proposition. The problem of unpredictability and the prospect of failure does not and has not ever worried me in the slightest – except no one likes to see a group missing the target or even falling completely flat on their faces – that's not a problem.

Twenty to twenty-five per cent of our programme arises from work in which we are on the ground floor at the stage of its birth, where we're either commissioning it or saying, 'What's your next project?' because we're interested. It's a mixture of that and anything clearly of absolutely landmark quality which we feel must be seen in this country, either for the sake of the artists who are producing it or for the sake of the audience or, a very close necessity, for the sake of the artists who are naturally part of our public. This is, I suppose, a potentially contentious point: sometimes our audience can consist quite largely of artists. I have very little difficulty with that. I think it is important that artists play to artists and people have that kind of opportunity to see which may spill over in their own work.

There is a sense in which Tramway has been very deliberately trying to show people work which is as good as it gets or as innovative as it gets, just to remind us that there are other ways of skinning a cat, so to speak. The Maly residency in May is probably the stiffest go we've had at that, by bringing five different plays, eight productions in total, so people really can get to grips with how that sort of repertoire system works and the education and training which underlines and supports it.

I think also there is another thing which is really to do with what a producer **is**. I still think that's a new area for a lot of British theatre. We tend to divide people into the artist who made the work, the director who directs it and other people who are **administrators**, but I think the producer figure is one which, again, is much more common abroad, quite different and a mixture of both.

I always define the producer as an incomplete artist. You often find with producers that they've been artists or they have a very profound training in an art form. They have the judgement of an artist, they have the receptivity of an artist, they can be moved or stimulated by things just as any artist can. They can even think like an artist, they certainly know better work from bad. The only thing is they can't make the stuff, they just can't do it. And where you get that kind of sensibility with a tremendous flair for organisation and particularly a flair for resource-finding, then you've got a very powerful combination of strengths in an individual or an institution, someone who really responds to an artistic idea and says: Follow me, I know just exactly how we're going to make that happen.

I wish we had more of them. People like Brian McMaster and Gavin Henderson, Rose Fenton and Lucy Neal are very impressive individuals in their own right. These are deeply creative individuals. Although she works on a very small scale I think Nikki Milican and what she has done with the National Revue of Live Art and New Moves is perhaps the strongest example of what I call a pure producer. She doesn't do anything else, virtually, except help the artists who most need it, i.e., the tiny independent groups who work with virtually no money, who work without any kind of context of support at all, she's the one who helps them develop. And the number of artists who've been through her hands – Lloyd Newson is an example, Forced Entertainment have benefited from her, all of the groups who came out of the Impact Theatre Co-operative, Steve Shill, all these people . . . And there are others – Val Bourne, John Ashford, Lois Keidan . . .

I cannot emphasise enough the potential creativity of that role. They do have these things in common: they tend to be anonymous, they're the unsung people; they tend to be highly mobile, they get to see a lot of work, they sort of absorb a lot of the techniques and the ideas and the practices that they see; they're often brilliant advisers, great at holding the hands of artists who may be unsure of what to do next or how to put an idea into action. And they work their butts off. Very important.

You do a lot of travelling and get to see a large amount of theatre in Europe and beyond. What kind of perspective does this give you on the British theatrical landscape at the moment? Where do we fit in, where are we going?

It's so difficult to know where to enter this issue. Because on the one hand the optimist in me says that there's just some great work happening, that's just a fact. There's great work happening at the National and the RSC, great work happening with some of the companies who don't have a building base, there are some of the repertory companies who are doing incredibly well . . . And part of me thinks – when I'm not being optimistic – that the British public, the community at large, is getting better than it deserves to get, given the treatment that is being meted out to the theatremakers.

The more I travel, the more awash I am with admiration at how people here manage to produce work on three-, four-week rehearsal periods of a standard which can occasionally equal anything in the world. And the more astonished I am at what miracles are being worked financially. There is no theatre economy with comparable problems to the British theatre economy **in the world** as far as I can see – in the developed world, where the idea of the public culture supporting theatremaking is taken for granted. There just isn't one. I think Britain represents at its best a miracle of survival, against market odds, against political odds and so on.

However, I still feel something which is generally true of a large part of our theatrical mainstream is that we are suffering more and more from cultural and creative isolation. I think the root of this is . . . There are two things: we are still, for whatever reason, whether it's self-inflicted, whether it's part of our thousand-year-old history, whether it's to do with the richness of our heritage, the global power of the language, a mixture of all, I think – we are living and working with our theatrical sensibilities **enclosed**. It's a kind of quarantine. The British theatre community has rarely thought it necessary to travel professionally. And the lack of a habit of interaction has I think been at enormous cost to the development of our work **dramaturgically**.

This is the second point that worries me: generally speaking, we operate in a dramaturgical vacuum in the British theatre, particularly in the more mainstream theatres where we're talking about companies who are staging texts. The way in which a group of artists, led by a director, reaches a point of view, hones ideas in, hones ideas out, tries to see itself as building up a body of work, a kind of mature approach to staging contemporary text or classical text – it hardly exists. I think that we're terribly impoverished by that. I think that directors could make things much easier for themselves if they were to look for support amongst thinkers . . . The dramaturg is a profession which is hardly known here.

On the other hand I may defend them also: when you're worrying about whether you're going to make 62% with this production, when you're worrying about getting the thing on in three weeks, when you're worrying about a designer screaming for another £2,000 to give you what you want, etcetera etcetera etcetera . . . what use is a dramaturg in all of that? To me this lack of a systematic way of introducing and sustaining clear thought, clear purpose into the whole interpretative process is another victim of the kind of working conditions we've been talking about. If people were to make the trip, particularly at the moment to the Netherlands or to Flanders, I think they'd be astonished at the relative distance that theatremakers have travelled. The theatre vocabulary of the average production in front of the 'average' Dutch audience or French audience is so much more sophisticated. There's a much stronger set of ideals at play in this kind of work – about the art form, or about what the text is conveying or ideals as grand as the role of the theatre artist in society.

And it just can't be separated from the financial issue. Directors and companies in these countries have got more time to do things. They can perhaps afford to be more radical in what they do, they can afford to lose the interest and the support of the public from time to time. But let me say that is **not** happening. You can see the most difficult work being presented in the Netherlands or Flanders, parts of Germany to some extent or at festivals, where there's a clear sense that theatremakers have taken a loyal public with them – so that maybe the public don't even know what a theatre risk **is** any longer.

All we do in Britain is worry about that: we talk about it, we worry about it and very few people actually **do** it. I believe that our state of divorce from continental practice has got a lot to do with it.

And it's something that the audiences there are educated in. If they read bad reviews, they go along and make up their own minds.

That's correct, though bad shows don't routinely sell out! I think that what I'm really saying is that at its worst, mainstream British theatre has broken down into a **service** for **markets**. That is the avenue down which it has been forced. Forced down it by funding-body thinking. Funding bodies are obsessed with theatrical categories in this country: YPT, children's theatre, puppets, movement theatre, dance, mime, small-scale touring, mid-scale touring, lyrical touring, repertory theatres, studio theatres, interdisciplinary work . . .

If we have a malaise, I don't believe it is completely self-inflicted. The British theatre has been chopped up, not just by dismal political ignorance, but also by people who want to fund it in a particular way **and only that way**. So it doesn't matter how creative or inspiring an artist can be, a director of a repertory theatre will have great difficulty in breaking out of that box, they really will think I'm main scale or I'm rep, so doing this is probably not open to me. So it actually restricts the capacity to turn the best of their imaginations into three dimensions. I really believe that.

I feel despite, maybe even because of, all the difficulties and our increased awareness of them, it is actually a very interesting time.

It is an exciting time. Look at the changes which **have** been made: Nottingham Playhouse, Salisbury Playhouse, Neil Bartlett at the Lyric . . . For one thing the cry of not enough money and poor resources is beginning to be seen for what it is, which is **no real excuse** for finding the undoubted talent which is out there, the revolutionary talent. I feel that there's now an inkling that the new talents amongst us are outstanding, and in place of the kinds of revolutions which made the late sixties exciting, which you must admit were associated with what the French would call *grands travaux* like the creation of the RSC, the creation of a new National Theatre . . .

And the English Stage Company playing to 20%.

And not worrying about it! All of that. I wonder whether what we're watching is the decline of the **playgoer**. I think the playgoer is a declining breed. The number of people who go to see the well-crafted play text, brilliantly interpreted and all the rest of it . . . I think in a way that's no longer **enough**. It's not going to regenerate an audience, because there are audiences now who are much more interested in experience. They're much more interested in the power of an experience that a great theatre production can deliver which can be had from no other art form.

Maybe what we're seeing now is a slow marrying of those ideas. Theatremakers who are more interested in bending the form this way and that and seeing whether it will survive the contortion are at last now being invited to work on the main stages or even taking them over. So much of what is to come is a matter of chance, because we don't know whether these talents will stick around.

It's also a matter of politics. There's just no question that the theatre community can continue to be unravelled slowly as is being done. Someone, sometime soon, is going to have to take the whole garment and shred it, and say: OK, there are the bits, now put back what you can out of that, and see what it looks like, try it on, see if it fits. We **just** got away with it this year, with the decision for equal misery for all instead of closing those ten theatres. That just won't go on if the Government carries on meting out the treatment it is.

And when I think of people like Ruth MacKenzie and her colleagues running Nottingham Playhouse – I remember Ruth when she was running a pick-up company called Moving Parts of about eight actors who were being paid £20 a week to come to Lincolnshire to sleep on my cottage floor, doing three shows a day – those are people who've **always** made work on no resources. And that's new, you see. I think that's new and very exciting. It's the people who've always been good at conjuring brilliant things out of virtually nothing, might be able to produce the same miracles on virtually something.

These questions about new direction, vision, risk, are general, but they take very distinct individual forms: Who is going to take over from Richard Eyre? Is it right for Nottingham Playhouse to present dance? Can the Wrestling School now have a Barker text co-produced abroad in three countries and get away with it? And can it lead to other things? Can these questions be faced? Of course they can. What we may see is the demise of the building. We may end up having fewer buildings than we've had before, which attacks the article of faith that 'every town should have one'. But so many of those towns have just been using them as 3-D cinema or 3-D television or a way of trying to get people to pass the time – is that a great loss?

gloria
Wanting to reclaim British theatre

Gloria was formed in 1988 to produce the work of four
artists: Neil Bartlett, Nicolas Bloomfield, Leah
Hausman and Simon Mellor. They work together as
writer/director; composer; director/choreographer and
producer respectively. There have been ten Gloria
productions, including: *A Vision of Love Revealed in
Sleep Part Three* (1989), *Sarrasine* (1990), *A
Judgement in Stone* (1992) and *Night After Night*
(1993). In April 1994 the company began a new
creative partnership with the Lyric Theatre,
Hammersmith, with the appointments of Neil Bartlett
as Artistic Director and Simon Mellor as Administrative
Producer. Nicolas Bloomfield and Leah Hausman were
prevented from attending our interview at
the last minute.

Left to right: Neil Bartlett, Leah Hausman, Simon Mellor and Nicolas Bloomfield.

Gloria's been going for six years now. Are you still surprised you're all together?

NEIL BARTLETT: We've been working together much longer than that. Nick and I did our first show together in 1979.

SIMON MELLOR: **We** started working together in '82.

NB: And I did my first work with Leah in '83.

SM: We were almost always creating solo work or small-scale work and very much throwing things together. Gloria was set up basically to raise money, to make our work happen. We didn't actually think at that time that we would necessarily be working together on projects. What became clear as we did start working together was that what we enjoyed most was to work all together on all our shows. It doesn't seem to me at all odd that we're still all working together. It seems completely logical.

But the important thing, I guess, is that Gloria is a part-time company in that Leah does quite a lot of work outside the company, I've always done bits and pieces of other work, Neil's had other writing projects . . .

NB: Yes. It isn't the only thing we do.

SM: And that keeps us quite bubbly I think, quite alive.

It's also a company which you formed at quite a mature stage in your collective careers.

SM: We set up Gloria with a very clear agenda for ourselves. We felt that we'd got to a certain stage in the theatre establishment, a certain level where we were confined inevitably to end up playing small-scale black-box art houses. Even in 1988 we knew that we wanted to get into mainstream theatre.

NB: We didn't want to play black boxes because every time we do, we spend all the creative energy we've got to make the audience have an experience which isn't about sitting in a black box but which is about **theatre**. We used lots of spaces for our earlier work. By the time we set up Gloria, Nick and I had done pieces in the street, in somebody's bathroom, in Oscar Wilde's old living room, then with Complicite again in the street, schools, everywhere. And then we took *Lady Audley's Secret* to Hamburg. We were playing in a nineteenth-century vaudeville theatre and we all just went:

Ohh, it's so beautiful! And suddenly no one asked us why we moved like that or why we had all that music because this was its **home.**

SM: That was quite odd for us because we'd come through a way of thinking and a way of working which was that those theatres were bad, they were the problem.

NB: They belonged to our parents.

SM: We had to get into those black boxes and that's where the radical work had to happen and that's where the really diverse audiences happen. And what we began to learn is that's nonsense. Those black boxes actually attract a much, much more homogenous audience than municipal theatres do. The town rep has a much broader range of audience than the arts centre. Who we play to has always been one of the things that we've talked a lot about.

NB: And actually in the work as well as in the office. The work often talks about: Who am I looking at? Who am I talking to? Oh, you're different to you . . . And no one was talking about those things.

SM: Most of our peers were not talking about the things that we loved, which was grand theatre traditions: melodrama and opera and music-hall . . .

NB: And musicals. And drag shows.

SM: Everyone was looking to Paris or to Eastern Europe and that whole kind of European art tradition. We were increasingly interested in how you reclaim the theatre traditions of **this** country.

NB: Steve Rogers asked me to edit an issue of *Performance* magazine and I went straight off and interviewed David Freeman and Lily Savage. That was quite a turning point in my thinking, about the things that we were talking about and the things that we were enjoying. Companies that do devised work characteristically always have a period where you assemble your sources. And our sources were not in Paris and they weren't in Germany. They were in the Vauxhall and they were at the Coliseum. They were increasingly in music and musicals.

SM: I always remember seeing some of Rose English's shows very early and thinking: Oh, right! She's the only other person . . .

NB: . . . Who transformed those spaces into theatres. I remember Rose's show at Theatre Workshop, *The Bridge*: wonderful, wonderful. And thinking, this could be in a theatre and she **wants** it to be. And the incredible triumph when she did that show in the Hackney Empire, which seemed like a real vindication of that.

Your work does seem to be very British – even in something like the name Gloria, which is this wonderful combination of Latin and what you imagine as this blonde barmaid with a rather large chest . . .

NB: Absolutely! Classic but cheap!

This mixture of erudition and trash is something which I think is fairly peculiar to this country. And what I admire very much about your work is that you take it very seriously on an artistic level but it has to be fun. **Lots and lots of fun.**

SM: There's always been this notion that somehow you have entertainment and then you have art.

NB: We've never experienced that division. We did a comparison exercise between Pina Bausch's *1980* and *Follies* and why you love them **both**. Because you can describe them both in the same way: it's multi-disciplinary theatre, it does this extraordinary thing of using the real age or the real physiques of the performers in a very emotive collision with idealised physiques and idealised theatre voices. And it has an almost incomprehensible cut-up structure which is totally comprehensible. And it's packed and people cry and people laugh. And they take place in big theatres. And there are incredible moments where thirty people do one thing together and you just rise to it. All of those things apply equally to *1980* and to *Follies* and those two works are very important to all four of us.

SM: I think it's also this thing of really wanting to reclaim British theatre. I always remember someone – I don't know if it was John Ashford – saying if Pina Bausch worked in Britain she'd be doing a one-woman show in the Oval House. And that's absolutely right. Where are the people who really want to work in the big theatres and that are prepared to have a strategy to get into them? There's no point in saying: Why won't you let us in there?

NB: We've been having this conversation for ten years. There are still lots of meetings, articles, seminars, conferences about why, why won't you let us into those spaces. What letting us into those spaces basically means is giving us huge amounts of money. And we've increasingly made it our business to find out about how that world works. I think people don't talk enough about the practicalities here. Why isn't there more large-scale original music theatre? Well, you have to know how much it costs and how you can devise a project which will justify that expenditure.

SM: I think it's got a lot to do with the fact that most people don't ask themselves any questions about why people go to the theatre. Why do people go to the theatre in the 1990s? There's still this thing of 'We make art and that's all that matters and we should be given the opportunity and the facility to make art in whatever space we choose to make it' – rather than saying: Why should people come and see the work we make? How do you create work which can survive commercially within that world? There is a whole economic and financial construction there. I suppose that's one of the ways that the company's organised – that my input, which isn't just purely financial but obviously has that element, is a central part of it when we talk about our shows. We talk about where we're going to perform it, who's going to come to it, how do we finance it, what are the economics of it, those sorts of arguments and issues are central **artistically**.

NB: We were taught very actively through the eighties that that's mainstream-speak. That's automatically a betrayal. And that's not our experience – you know, that there's an automatic antagonism between the budget and the art.

Can I come back to one of the things that you were saying about Pina Bausch and *Follies*, about you having a very clear sense of the works being tailored to particular performers and you had a very real sense of them being on stage together with their aspirations to be something which is not them. Because that's a quality in the shows that I've seen of Gloria's that's very powerful and there's a real energy there.

NB: Well, the reason that that happens and why people see that in our work is for a really specific reason. We started off in a working environment where you had the personnel before you had the show. It's the classic model of all those companies performing devised work. And that's the opposite of the way that work is conventionally produced, where you have the script first and where you cast it. And when we make shows, we assemble the performers first so that the work is literally made **for** as well as with the performers concerned. We wanted to write *A Judgement in Stone* for Sheila Hancock, who is perceived to be one of the most loved and loving of popular artists, to perform a role of someone who literally couldn't spell the word love, had never experienced it, to whom it was an impossible concept. It was incredibly poignant to see somebody who everyone loved playing someone who nobody loved. And what's best about our work is what comes out of a very close collaboration with individual performers.

SM: It's also a recognition that the reason why most people go to the theatre is to see someone do something special. And we talk about that a lot. You have to take that on board. People like Sheila Hancock or Bette Bourne are the most incredibly technically accomplished performers. And they never do the same performance twice.

When I think about it all those things that are talked about in the Gaulier–Lecoq world: that you respond to the audience, that it's always a live performance – those things are always present in one of their performances. But what was delicious was they also brought with them a whole other tradition which excited us, the fact that Sheila had been in *Sweeney Todd*, *Oliver* and all those wonderful shows.

That's why we choose to work with those sorts of performers. We like them to have a sense of character that they've brought from offstage onto the stage and I think that's why when our shows work you think: This is no longer that character speaking, it's that person now, it's that performer now, talking to me. And I always feel our work works best at that moment.

NB: That's what the work's **about**: why that moment happens. It is that incredible thing of seeing Eartha Kitt in *Follies*: halfway through the second verse, you went: She is singing 'I'm still here' and **she's** still here and that is **her** fur coat that she's wearing and look where she started, and suddenly you went: Oh!, and you didn't even begin to imagine that, you know, a musical at the Shaftesbury in the West End could be about those things – and it **was** about those things. And the audience rose to its feet because it was about those things, not because they were going: This is a really nice song in a musical.

And I did get a very clear sense sitting in *Night After Night* of knowing those people – or I felt that I did. That may be very sophisticated artifice . . .

NB: Of course it's a trick! It's a technique. Yes. Because the cast of *Night After Night* were deeply private, guarded people. They don't walk in and go: Hi, I'd really like to expose my soul to you now. It takes a long time to be that straightforward. (*Laughs.*)

On the other hand, presenting shows through your own persona is something you have quite a lot of experience in now. Is this something that you find gets easier?

NB: No.

SM: It feels like each show gets harder to make. But that's because we set ourselves more difficult tasks each time.

NB: Making *A Vision of Love Revealed in Sleep* was child's play compared to making *Night After Night* because *A Vision of Love Revealed in Sleep* fitted into a suitcase. I made it on my own. I created that show by locking myself into a room, next door to a studio where Robin Whitmore was painting, also locked into a room. We'd meet once a day. And that work structure of course is an absolute doddle compared to *Night After Night* which had a band and things flying down from the ceiling and thirty-seven costume changes . . . It had a ballet in it, for God's sake! All those things were incredibly difficult to do. So that gets harder. The things that I want to say don't **feel** any harder but I think the things I want to say now are harder to say, they're probably more complicated.

SM: We get better about knowing about the system for making work on this scale. When we first started, the notion of having a stage manager was an incredible luxury and now suddenly we've got three or four of them.

NB: You've been working for ten years and then you realise that most people don't build their own sets! And – Simon will tell you – I still have incredible problems with that. Given half the chance, I would design, build and paint all our own sets because that's where I'm still coming from. But you learn. You learn that there are colleagues who can do things that you can't do. So you work with them. That's the reason why you work with other people.

Sometimes you do wake up in the middle of the night and you go: Oh, let's do a devised two-person show on a small-scale tour.

SM: But we've always really enjoyed the grind of learning how you work in the British theatre system. For an experimental new company who does new music theatre, we do over a hundred performances a year. Now that's a lot.

Are you conscious, in seeking out a bigger audience, that the work is changing?

SM: Yes. When you make a decision that you want to play in five-hundred-seat theatres, there's no point in pretending you can play *Sarrasine* in a five-hundred-seat theatre or *A Vision of Love*. You do have to go: What are the elements that make it marketable? The fact that we're doing a new piece of gay music theatre in a five-hundred-seat theatre here and in Nottingham and in Manchester and in Leeds is only possible because it's called *The Picture of Dorian Gray* and it's got Maria Aitken in it. I think that's one of the things that people from our background sometimes don't really address.

NB: It's really important to understand that we've chosen. I could still be touring the solo version of *A Vision of Love Revealed in Sleep*. I'm still asked to do that. I could be doing that.

SM: The other solution that a lot of our peers chose is international work. Partly because we can't reassemble the sorts of companies that we've got but also if you want to use text a lot – as we do – that becomes much harder.

NB: Also, I have a big problem with fraudulent relationships with the audience, where the audience is there telling themselves that they are having a direct and dynamic communication with a work of art which is coming from a culture very different from theirs. As a member of the audience I've had too many experiences of art soup, where this event which has come in for two days is wonderful but I am not plugged into it and it is not plugged into me. And I sit there and I wonder why everyone is saying that they think it is.

I felt absolutely split about Peter Sellars' *The Persians*, which I found enormously impressive and pleasurable, because half of me is going: I really am seeing those performers on this bare stage getting this story over to me!

And the other half of me is going: I know how much this cost! It cost almost as much as the war it is describing! And I have a problem with people saying: Isn't it incredible to sense an audience drawn into the community of feeling in this piece?, when they know that eighty per cent of that audience came to this show on a plane.

SM: That's a classic example of a show which was not made for any audience. We know the way it was made. And I don't think that question was ever asked: Who is going to come and see this show? Who is this show for? And we ask ourselves that question a lot: Who is this show for? Why are we making this show? Why would they want to come and see it? What does it mean to them?

NB: And then people go: Oh, why don't we have shows like that in this country? Sound of Neil dropping off perch! (*Laughs.*) We should **know** straight away why we don't have shows like that in this country.

Your interest in British theatre is one which places you in a tradition. Though your work is consciously experimental, at the same time it's trying to find a continuity with the past.

NB: I think my work is very full of ghosts. There are often dead people in my work and there are often quotations from the past in my work and the same with Nicolas. His music is haunted by a history which he then reinvents as he's writing. Leah's work is full of ghosts in that it's informed by her understanding and experience of a ballet training and specifically an American ballet training. We've all got that in common and therefore it seems to me entirely logical that we would work in **buildings** that have ghosts.

And that's precisely why we want to make work here. I like to make work in spaces which are very crowded. My rehearsal rooms and work studios are always very crowded. I'm always going in and sticking up little bits of old stuff on the walls. My scrapbooks are always very crowded and when we're preparing for a work our ears are crowded with music and therefore to work in those buildings is important.

And it's one reason why you've now come to the Lyric Theatre and are doing lyric theatre.

SM: A very ghostly building. Yes. It's the ghosts here that excite us. But I think it's also important to say you can make new work in these spaces.

NB: And the other place where those ghosts exist is in the minds and eyes of the people who come to see the shows. That's something that's really important. We really enjoy the older audience that is now starting to come to our work as well as the younger audience. And it freaks me out in the most wonderful way when Sandy Wilson came to see *Night After Night*: he's seeing this work through his eyes and – he told us about it – all these other shows, all these other performers are running across in front of him. And that's amazing. And some of the performers that we've talked about – everybody in *Night After Night* – you felt that they were incredibly themselves but also, in some way you couldn't put your finger on, they had a lot of other people's stories and other people's techniques and they'd been in a lot of shows.

You were talking about the audience of older people. How important is it to you to produce work which is informed by your own sexuality and present it to a variety of audiences, some of whom are gay and some aren't? Is that an important agenda – or is that something that you stop thinking about?

SM: No, he can't help himself.

NB: It just comes out! (*Laughs.*) No, you can't ever stop thinking about it because if you're on tour there are managers, within the media there are critics, there are performers: there are people all over the business who still think that if the work is made by a gay person, that work will be limited. And you mustn't stop thinking about those people because you mustn't let them get away with that. You mustn't let them carry the argument because their argument is nonsense.

I don't talk about it very much because the thing is that we're getting there but it can be taken away at a moment's notice. If I announced that the first piece that I was going to do here was a big fag piece, then there'd be trouble – from all quarters. As it happens, the first piece that I'm going to do here **is** a big fag piece but it's not being talked about in that way and that's very deliberate and that's very right and I'm in control of it.

SM: It's very interesting when you talk to people about Neil's work and they go: He's this gay theatremaker – especially when we did *Night After Night*, people said: It's just like his last show. And they meant *Sarrasine*. Actually he's done five shows since then.

NB: Personally I think my **really** faggy work was *The Game of Love and Chance*. I blush at the queerness of that show, but no one sort of spotted it . . . The most powerful influence on the writing of *Night After Night* was the dialogue between Leah and myself. Because I suggested the idea of the child playing his own parent and then the person who directed it is a mother. And the whole show spins on the central *pas de deux* – and that's Leah's piece of work. And that's very important that we say that, because Leah's not here. It's very interesting for people to look at *Night After Night* again, take me out of it, and watch it as a show choreographed by a woman with a son. That's very revealing. It's also coming into *Dorian Gray* very much again.

Absolutely. I saw it in Edinburgh when my wife was pregnant and I felt I could relate to it very deeply on a particular level . . .

NB: A lot of people did.

. . . and really got a great deal out of it that way. Having said that, I know a number of gay people who work in the theatre whose sexuality is not reflected in their work at all.

NB: The reason why I think it's in my work and in Nick's work is because we're actually influenced formally by what we think of as an actual tradition of gay theatre. I talk about the tradition of gay theatre in the same way that Leah talks about the tradition of American choreography. I think it's got a history, I think it's got landmarks, I think it's got twists and turns and I know about them. I've spent a great deal of time finding out about them. And I'm very influenced technically in the way that I animate the stage, in the way that I perform.

I am very influenced by Ethyl Eichelberger and the work of the Ridiculous Theatrical Company and by Lily Savage and by Regina Fong and by Bette Bourne and the work of the Bloolips. I'm very influenced by the work of Rattigan and Novello and Coward and I'm very informed by all that. And I think that that's what's missing in other people's work.

We think – because we've been told – that homosexuality in the theatre was invented about 1969 – depending on which book you're reading – and that the way in which it was invented was as **subject matter**. I don't think that homosexuality is a subject. I think it's an aesthetic tradition which is as complicated and as wonderful and also as redundant as classical ballet. And I want to be part of that tradition. And so that's the difference, from where I'm standing. You can have a play which has gay characters in it, but from where I'm sitting it's not remotely gay.

SM: It's back to that thing of ghosts and reinvention. It's what our work is about, it's about taking a history of theatrical form and musical form and re-exploring it and re-examining it. All our shows are about a dialogue between the present and the past, really. They all have that device where something happens in one time frame and there's something else happening in another time frame.

NB: And it's also happening now. Because you're watching it.

You've just taken over this very beautiful theatre: what sort of hopes and plans do you have for the future?

SM: I hope that we're going to be able to be planning our next season here at the Lyric in a year's time. Sometimes it feels like that will be an incredible achievement . . .

NB: It **will** be an incredible achievement.

SM: . . . to get through a year and have put together the season of work we're putting together and have paid our way at the box office so we're in a position to do it again. That seems very hard to do in Britain at the moment. You don't really have opportunities to fail any longer. You've got to get it right first time and everyone finds that very hard and I think that's why less and less people want to work in buildings.

We've just gone through an astonishingly successful fundraising campaign here – I never thought we would do it – £325,000 in five months. And we know we'll never get a chance to do it again. We have to make our season work. And that's frightening and exciting.

NB: I'd like to be able to get this building to a point where we can afford live music on a regular basis. Because I am fascinated by what was done here, I am fascinated by why this was the auditorium in London where Gay and

Britten and Offenbach and revues were done. And I would love a chance to explore the aesthetics of that. And we'll only be able to do that if we turn the finances of the building round. So that's why I'm prepared to do all this **work**, so that we might have a chance of doing some of those pieces.

Gloria has a little box with four more shows in it. I really want to do those four shows. I also want to do *Lady in the Dark*. Then, when we've done all that, I can do *Athalie* by Racine – that's what I **really** want to do. But I can wait a long time before doing that.

SM: Having ideas for shows has never been our problem. It's getting to the position where you feel like you've **earned the right** to do the work. We always feel that's what we go through. We feel we don't have a right, we have to earn it. And that's really true here. You can only do certain types of shows here if you know you've earned it.

What about your studio? Do you think there are people you can get to come in there who are in the sort of position that Gloria was in six years ago?

NB: I hope there are some people that we can take into the main house. I'm doing a show in the main house with Emily Woof next spring, for instance. And Emily's position now is not dissimilar to where we were in '87/'88. I think her work is better than ours was in that period, which is why I want her to come into the main house with me. And I'm looking very carefully at the area of young designers and I think that there's quite a good argument that visual artists, if you're on the right project, could go into the main house. And that's a very important part of our work.

SM: And we're going to be working on a show with Forkbeard Fantasy, who are a British experimental theatre company who've been going twenty-five years. I think they've earned the right to play in the main house.

NB: Can't put them in the studio, that's for sure.

SM: It's that thing of saying to them: Why don't you work with us on a Christmas show? It's trying to find that dialogue, to take those artists and say: How can you make work which we can sell to five hundred people a night for five or six weeks? And that's the way we want to work: we do want to open doors.